It's another Quality Book from CGP

This book is for anyone studying AQA GCSE Graphic Products.

Let's face it, D&T is pretty hard-going — you've got a whole load of technical stuff to learn on top of doing your project.

Happily this CGP book helps to take the headache out of all that learning. We've explained all the technical stuff — and drawn plenty of pictures to make the whole thing that bit clearer. Plus we've stuck in some handy hints to help make your project a winner.

And in true CGP style it's got some daft bits in to try and make the whole experience at least vaguely entertaining for you.

What CGP is all about

Our sole aim here at CGP is to produce the highest quality books — carefully written, immaculately presented and dangerously close to being funny.

Then we work our socks off to get them out to you — at the cheapest possible prices.

Contents

Published by CGP

Editors:
Katie Braid, Katherine Craig, Ben Fletcher, Rosie Gillham, Sarah Hilton,
Adam Moorhouse, Hayley Thompson.

Contributors:
Catherine Atsiaris, Ryan Ball, Debbie McGrory, Janice Donoghue,
Juliet Gibson, Stephen Guinness, Alan Nanson, Anthony Wilcock.

With thanks to Ryan Ball for the content review.
With thanks to Paul Jordin, Sharon Keeley and Fiona Leyman for the proofreading.

With thanks to Laura Stoney for the copyright research.

ISBN: 978 1 84762 356 0

Groovy website: www.cgpbooks.co.uk
Jolly bits of clipart from CorelDRAW®

With thanks to iStockphoto® for permission to use the lemon squeezer image on page 6.

The motorway sign image on page 6 is reproduced under the terms of Crown Copyright Policy Guidance issued by HMSO.

With thanks to BSI for permission to reproduce the Kitemark symbol on page 59.
Kitemark and the Kitemark symbol are registered trademarks of BSI.
For more information visit www.kitemark.com.

With thanks to the Forest Stewardship Council for permission to reproduce the logo on page 57,
©1996 Forest Stewardship Council A.C.

With thanks to The British Toy & Hobby Association for permission to reproduce the Lion Mark logo on page 59.

Every effort has been made to locate copyright holders and obtain permission to reproduce sources.
For those sources where it has been difficult to trace the originator of the work, we would be grateful for
information. If any copyright holder would like us to make an amendment to the acknowledgements,
please notify us and we will gladly update the book at the next reprint. Thank you.

Printed by Elanders Ltd, Newcastle upon Tyne.

Based on the classic CGP style created by Richard Parsons.

Project Advice

Unlike most subjects, in D&T you actually get to make something useful (well, hopefully).

The Project is Worth 60% of your GCSE

1) Your D&T project is called 'the controlled assessment'.

2) Your teacher will give you as much help as they're allowed to by the exam board, so do ask them... but mostly it's up to you to make a good job of your project.

3) You can dip into this book for a bit of extra help. Section 1 is all about the design process, so if you're not sure where to start, that might be a good place to look.

4) If you're wondering about a particular detail — what type of adhesive to use, say — it's probably quickest to look it up in the index and go straight to those pages.

Only Put Relevant Stuff in your Folder

Your teacher will give you plenty of guidance on what needs to go in your folder, but here are some tips:

1) The folder should be approximately 20 sheets of A3. You'll lose marks if you do much more.

2) So DON'T waste space on irrelevant stuff, especially at the research stage. For example:

> Say you've analysed some existing restaurant menus, looking at how they were finished...
>
> Don't bore the examiners stupid with detailed descriptions of the menus from every restaurant within a ten mile radius of your school.
>
> A brief summary of your research findings is all that's needed — then the really important thing to say is how those findings helped you decide how to finish your product.

3) DO put in lots of photos. The examiners love this. They want to see photos of:

- Any models you make (see p.10). Don't just put in photos of the ones that worked. In fact, the ones that didn't quite work are more useful because then you can explain what was wrong and how you fixed it.

- The intermediate stages of making your final product — part of the way through the assembly process, say — to show how you constructed it.

4) CHECK that you've used the right technical words and spelled things correctly. And make sure you've explained things clearly — get someone who knows nothing about your project to read it and see if it makes sense.

Here's me with the manufacturing specification.

The Exam is Worth 40%

1) In the exam you'll be tested on everything you've learned during the course — materials, tools, how to design things, how to make things, health and safety, environmental issues...

2) This book can help you learn all that stuff — and has questions for you to check what you know.

3) There's a glossary at the back of the book (pages 82-84), in case you need to sort out your mock-ups from your models.

4) The exam technique section (pages 78-81) has some worked examples of exam-style questions, and some hints on how to make sure you get top marks.

Controlled Assessment — nope, it's not funny...

When your project is marked, only about a third of the marks are for the final thing you've made and how good it is. Most of the controlled assessment marks depend on the sheer brilliance of your folder.

Product Life-Cycle

Graphic Products isn't just about drawing stuff. It's about making useful and attractive products. And just like butterflies, graphic products have a life-cycle — which you need to know about.

Find a Gap in the Market...

1) The design process often starts when someone finds a gap in the market. This is an area where there aren't products available to meet people's needs. For example, there aren't many pop-up recipe books.

2) The next stage is to hire a designer — and they design a new product to fill the gap.

3) The new product then needs to be manufactured and sold. Simple.

Tim's Mum had to tell him there weren't any pop-up recipe books available.

...And Decide Who Your Target Group is

It's important to work out what group of people you want to sell your product to — the target market. You can group people by things like age, gender, job, hobbies, how rich they are...

> For example... the target market for pop-up recipe books is probably the parents of young children who are interested in cooking.

1) You need to design the product with the target group in mind (see p.8-9)...

2) ...and aim your marketing (advertising, free samples, etc) at them.

Every Product Has a Life-Cycle

So, someone identifies a gap in the market for a new product. The product is designed, manufactured and put on sale, aimed firmly at the target market. The pattern of sales usually goes something like this:

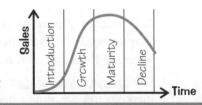

INTRODUCTION

The new product is launched (sold for the first time). Launching a new design is expensive — you have to pay the designer and spend a lot on marketing to persuade people to buy the product.

GROWTH

If the product's successful, sales go up, manufacturing costs go down (because you can mass-produce it) and so your profits increase. Competitors will start to introduce similar products.

DECLINE

The sales fall, and your profits shrink — and eventually the product is withdrawn from sale and replaced by a new one.

EVOLUTION

You could change the design a bit, to make it better, and re-launch it, OR it just declines...

MATURITY

When the product is well known, sales are high, but there are more competitors. So your product may have to be reduced in price, and there are fewer new customers.

Find the gap in the market — but don't fall down it...

Graphic products can be simple things like posters. But many graphic products are made by combining graphic materials (paper, board, ink, etc.) with other materials and components (plastic, velcro, rivets...)

Product Life-Cycle

Some Products Have Obsolescence Built In

If the stuff you bought lasted forever, there'd be no more jobs for designers and manufacturers. Luckily for them, that's not how it works. That product life-cycle just keeps on going, because:

1) Many products do eventually break.

2) Other products become so out of date that you can't use them (computers that are incompatible with new software, say) or you don't want to (because everyone else has newer, better stuff).

3) This stage — when a product is useless and the consumer has to replace it — is called obsolescence.

4) Sometimes designers deliberately design stuff so that it'll become useless quite quickly. This is called built-in obsolescence. Here are some ways to do it.

- Make the design poor quality — so the product breaks quickly.
- Design the product so it's impossible or really expensive to repair or update.
- Make the design really up to the minute — so that it's bound to become unfashionable quickly.

This has Advantages and Disadvantages

1) Built-in obsolescence drives innovation in new replacement products, and keeps designers and manufacturers in jobs.

2) But your customers might just get annoyed if they have to replace the product really soon, and never buy anything from you again.

3) Also, it's not great for the environment. You end up with mountains of thrown away products. And making all the replacement products uses up more resources and energy and often causes more pollution.

I've only had this calendar a year, and now it doesn't work at all...

Some Products are Designed for Maintenance

1) Some products would be really expensive or inconvenient to keep replacing.

2) Take road signs, for example — it'd be dangerous to keep taking them down and replacing them.

3) Your customers for products like this want them to be maintainable. E.g. road signs have surfaces that are easy to clean, and a panelled structure that's easy to repair.

Practice Questions

1) What is meant by a gap in the market?

2) a) What is a target market?
   b) Ryan is designing a 'Learn Your Alphabet' toy. What kind of people do you think should be his target market?

3) Sam has designed a mobile phone. It has just been released for sale. Outline the life-cycle stages that Sam should expect to see.

4) Julie has designed a board game with built-in obsolescence.
   a) What is meant by built-in obsolescence?
   b) Suggest some features that Julie's design could have to give it built-in obsolescence.
   c) Give one advantage and one disadvantage of built-in obsolescence.

5) Why are some products designed for maintenance?

Product Analysis

Designers often get <u>inspiration</u> by looking at <u>existing products</u>. Analysing the <u>good</u> and <u>bad</u> features of other people's designs can help you to make your <u>own</u> designs better, too.

Analyse Other Products — and Make Yours Better

1) When you're looking at an existing product, analyse how good the <u>design</u> is, and how well the product's been <u>made</u> (they're not the same thing — see next page). Think about all these things:

Is the <u>style</u> of the <u>text</u> and <u>pictures</u> suitable?

What kind of <u>customer</u> is it aimed at?

How much does it <u>cost</u>? Is it good value?

How's it been <u>constructed</u>?

Is it <u>safe</u>?

Is it the right <u>size</u>?

What's its <u>environmental impact</u>?

What <u>materials</u> is it made of?

How well does it get the intended <u>message</u> across?

Test it — does it do its <u>job well</u>?

2) Write down the product's <u>good points</u> and its <u>faults</u> — and say how to make your product <u>better</u>.

Ergonomic Designs Are Easy for People to Use

Good design includes making a product <u>easy</u> and <u>comfortable</u> for people to use — this is <u>ergonomics</u>.

1) **LETTERING** must be easy for the <u>target market</u> to <u>read</u>. For example, lettering for older people should not be too small, and the typeface for children's books should be especially large and clear.

2) Use **COLOUR** to achieve the effect you want. <u>Complementary colours</u> (see p.36) will make something <u>stand out</u>. Avoid relying on a contrast between red and green though — it won't be very clear for people who have red/green colour-blindness (the commonest kind). And if you want your design to be <u>easy on the eye</u>, use colours that are <u>close together</u> on the colour wheel (see p.36).

3) Products must be the right **SIZE AND SHAPE** for the intended users — see the next page.

4) If part of the product needs to be <u>gripped</u>, the **TEXTURE** might be important.

5) If the product needs to be <u>carried</u> or <u>moved</u> you'll need to keep its **WEIGHT** down by choosing the right <u>materials</u>.

Product Analysis — yep, mine's bigger than yours...

You'll probably be asked to <u>analyse designs</u> in the exam. That's your chance to talk about which features of the design are good or bad — and remember to say <u>why</u> ("I don't like it" doesn't count).

Product Analysis

Good Design and Good Manufacture are Different

A well-designed product:
- can carry out its <u>function</u> really well
- <u>looks</u> good and attracts consumers

A well-manufactured product:
- has been <u>made</u> to a <u>good standard</u> — things like the finish, folds, colour and material are all satisfactory
- is <u>accurate</u> to the original design

Anthropometric Data are Measurements of Humans

To make your product the <u>right size</u>, you need to know the likely <u>body measurements</u> of the <u>users</u>. Measurements of human body parts are called <u>anthropometric data</u>.

1) First, work out <u>what measurements</u> you need. For example, if your product is a novelty mask it doesn't matter how long the users' legs are — you only need to know about their heads.

2) <u>Find out</u> what these measurements are on the <u>typical user</u> of the product.
(The best way is to sample lots of people from the target group then take the average.)

3) Design your product to fit someone with <u>these average measurements</u>.

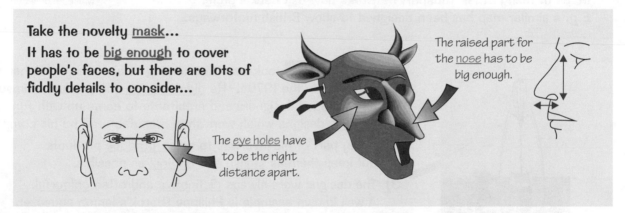

Take the novelty <u>mask</u>...
It has to be <u>big enough</u> to cover people's faces, but there are lots of fiddly details to consider...

The <u>eye holes</u> have to be the right distance apart.

The raised part for the <u>nose</u> has to be big enough.

4) BUT a product that fits <u>only</u> the <u>average</u> person <u>isn't</u> the best solution (most people <u>aren't</u> average).

5) So designers often aim to make the product fit <u>okay</u> for <u>90%</u> of the target users.
For example, they'd make the nose of the mask bigger than needed for the average nose.

Practice Questions

1) Sally has designed a <u>brochure</u> for her school open day. She wants her design to be <u>ergonomic</u>. Suggest <u>two</u> things she should think about.

2) Helen is designing a new <u>diary</u>. She starts by analysing <u>existing products</u>.
   a) Why is it important that she does this?
   b) Helen looks at the <u>design</u> and <u>manufacture</u> of the existing products.
      (i) Suggest two features of a <u>well designed</u> diary.
      (ii) Suggest two features of a <u>well made</u> diary.

3) a) What is <u>anthropometric data</u>?
   b) Suggest what anthropometric data would be needed for designing a <u>T-shirt</u>.

4) Calum has designed a drink-dispensing top hat to fit <u>90%</u> of his target market. Explain why he hasn't just used the <u>average measurements</u> of his target group.

Designers and What They Do

Being influenced by good designers is a great way to get ideas — and it doesn't count as copying either (unless you do just copy their stuff — that's against the law).

Recognise the Style of Influential Designers

There are a few designers you need to know about — they've all developed a style that has influenced other designers. They could influence your products too...

1) **Harry Beck** redesigned the London Underground map in the 1930s.

2) His map isn't geographically correct. It shows you which station comes next but the layout is very different from real life...

3) The map only has straight lines, running either vertically, horizontally or at 45°. (In reality the lines curve and wiggle all over the place.)

4) The stations are shown spaced out evenly (when actually some are much closer together than others).

5) As well as the simplified layout, each underground line is shown in a different colour — and station names are in the matching colour.

6) These features make it simple to use, and it's been a huge success. Maps of many other transport networks now use Beck's style. E.g. a similar map has been designed to show British motorways.

©TfL from the London Transport Museum collection.

1) **Alberto Alessi** took over the running of his family's kitchenware company in the 1970s. He didn't design any products himself — he employed designers and architects to come up with fun and creative designs which were then manufactured by his company.

2) A key part of his idea was to mass-produce products but keep them as stylish and original as possible.

3) The designs were always distinctive and often colourful. A well known example is Philippe Starck's lemon squeezer.

1) **Jock Kinneir and Margaret Calvert** were hired to design the new road signs needed when motorways were first opened in Great Britain.

2) Their signs had a simple map showing the road layout ahead. For the lettering, they developed a new typeface (font) which used curvy letters that were easier for drivers to read than older styles.

3) The signs were so easy to understand that their style was adapted for all the UK's other road signs, and by several other countries.

4) Kinneir and Calvert also developed the colour scheme for UK road signs, and they designed warning signs that used pictograms (see p.52).

Robert Sabuda developed a style of paper engineering — folding and cutting paper to create models that unfold and move. He's well known for creating pop-up books — many of his books have won awards. Many other people have produced pop-up books in a similar style.

Easy peasy lemon squeezy...

So, if you think you're cheating by looking at other designers' work, think again. You might be able to come up with a great new idea by focusing on something in their work. Just don't copy everything...

Designers and What They Do

Designers Can Help Create a Brand

1) It's important for large companies to develop their <u>brand</u> — this is the <u>image</u> that the public has of the company. (See page 54.)
2) Many companies employ <u>graphic designers</u> to create a <u>logo</u>, which helps people to <u>recognise</u> their brand.
3) Some companies employ <u>brand consultants</u> to help them build up the image they want. <u>Wally Olins</u> is thought to be one of the world's leading brand consultants. He's not a designer but he's worked with companies including BT and P&O, helping them to develop their brands.

Everyone recognises Farmer Jones' sheep now.

Designers Can Protect Their Designs

<u>Designers</u> don't want to spend time developing brilliant new products and then have other people come along and <u>copy</u> them. Fortunately there are several ways designers can <u>protect</u> their creations...

They can protect:
- the <u>appearance</u> of a product with <u>registered design</u>,
- any new <u>technology</u> they've invented with a <u>patent</u>,
- <u>logos</u> with a <u>trademark</u>,
- <u>text</u> or <u>images</u> by <u>copyright</u>.

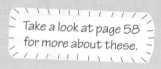

Take a look at page 58 for more about these.

Practice Questions

1) a) Who redesigned the <u>London Underground map</u> in the 1930s?
   b) What was different about this design from other maps?
   c) How has this design <u>influenced</u> other designs?

2) a) What was <u>Alberto Alessi's</u> 'big idea' for product design?
   b) Name a designer who has designed a product for the Alessi range.

3) a) What are <u>Kinneir and Calvert</u> well-known for doing?
   b) Suggest why their designs were a success.

4) a) What is <u>paper engineering</u>?
   b) What type of product that uses paper engineering is <u>Robert Sabuda</u> associated with?

5) a) What is meant by a '<u>brand</u>'?
   b) Why do many companies use a <u>logo</u>?
   c) Who is <u>Wally Olins</u>?

6) Carlo has designed a hand-held games console. How could he protect:
   a) his <u>logo</u>?
   b) the <u>appearance</u> of the product?
   c) the <u>text</u> and <u>diagrams</u> in the instruction booklet?

Design Briefs and Specifications

The best products are those that address a <u>real need</u>. The more people there are who would actually <u>use</u> a product, the more chance it stands of being a <u>roaring success</u>.

Designing Starts with the Design Brief

When someone gets an idea for a <u>new product</u>, they often <u>employ a designer</u> to work on the idea.

1) The person who hires the designer is called the <u>client</u>.

2) The <u>client</u> gives the designer a <u>design brief</u>...

3) The design brief is a <u>starting point</u> for the development of the product. It will probably include:

> • what <u>kind</u> of product is needed (and <u>why</u>)
> • how the product will be <u>used</u>
> • <u>who</u> the product is <u>for</u> (the <u>target market</u>)

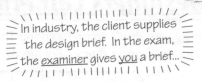

DESIGN BRIEF FOR STAPLE PACKAGING/WOODLOUSE HOUSE

No currently commercially available staple packaging has an in-built capacity for housing a pet woodlouse.
We want you to design a product to meet this need for those people who want to keep a pet after they've stapled their papers.

4) When the designer gets the design brief they'll start by <u>analysing</u> it — making sure they understand what the client wants.

5) Then they'll do lots of <u>research</u>.

In industry, the client supplies the design brief. In the exam, the examiner gives you a brief...

You'll Need to Do Some Research...

The research you do before designing your own product should include analysing <u>existing products</u> (see page 4). It also includes researching the <u>potential market</u> for the product.

1) The point of doing market research is to:

> • find out what people <u>like or dislike</u> about similar <u>existing products</u>
> • check that people will actually <u>want your product</u>

2) Even the best products won't be everyone's cup of tea — some people will <u>like</u> them and some <u>won't</u>.

3) Ask your <u>target market</u> what they want the product to be like.

4) You can ask <u>closed questions</u>, e.g. 'Which of these three fonts do you like best?'
   It's fairly easy to get <u>clear results</u> (and show them in graphs, etc.) with this type of question.

5) Or you can ask <u>open questions</u>, e.g. 'Why is Comic Sans MS your favourite font?'
   This kind of question is good if you want to get more <u>detail</u> about people's <u>opinions</u>.

...And Then Use Your Research to Draw Conclusions

Once you've done some <u>product analysis</u> and <u>market research</u>, you should have loads of information. Now you have to use the information to help with your design.

> 1) <u>Summarise</u> what you've found out — pick out the most important and useful findings.
>   E.g. 70% of people found it difficult to read text printed in size 10 Times New Roman font.
>
> 2) <u>Explain</u> what impact the research will have on your designs.
>   E.g. the font on my design should be size 12 or bigger.

This will help you write a <u>design specification</u> — see the next page...

Draw conclusions with research — not a pencil...

The rest of this section describes the <u>typical design process</u> that happens in industry. You need to understand the overall process even though you probably won't have to actually do every bit of it.

Design Briefs and Specifications

The Design Specification is a List of Conditions to Meet

1) The design specification gives certain <u>conditions</u> that the product must meet. These conditions should take account of your <u>research findings</u>.

> E.g. if you know that your target market would never buy a box of staples that costs more than £100, your design specification might include the statement, "Must cost £100 or less."

2) It's best to write a specification as <u>bullet points</u> rather than a paragraph of explanations. Include points to describe <u>some</u> or <u>all</u> of the following:

1. How it should look	4. Size
2. How it will be used	5. Safety points to consider
3. Materials, equipment and production method	6. Price range

Example:
- The packaging should weigh 80 g or less.
- It should be multicoloured.
- The maximum length will be 100 mm.
- The font should be size 12 or bigger.

EXAM TIP
In Section A of the exam you'll have to follow a specification to create a design.

3) The design specification acts as a <u>guide</u> to make sure that the product will do what you want it to — you <u>refer back to it</u> throughout the project.

4) So it's important that it's <u>clear and detailed</u> — the better it is, the more likely your product will be high quality.

Come Up With a Range of Design Ideas

EXAM TIP
Your initial ideas should be sketched freehand in pencil fairly quickly.

1) <u>Annotate</u> (add <u>notes</u> to) each idea to explain it fully.

2) <u>Check</u> that each design <u>matches</u> the <u>specification</u> — any that don't <u>won't</u> be <u>suitable</u>.

3) Also, check that you <u>could actually make</u> the designs. <u>Creativity</u> is a <u>splendid</u> thing... but total impracticality isn't.

4) Finally, choose <u>one</u> of your suitable designs to <u>develop further</u>.

Practice Questions

1) a) What information does a <u>design brief</u> include?
   b) In industry, who <u>writes</u> the design brief?

2) What's the point of doing <u>market research</u>?

3) Read these questionnaire results about fonts and write two brief <u>conclusions</u> based on them:

> Q1. Which colour font do you think the text looks best in?
> Answers: red: 9 black: 18 blue: 24 green: 6
> Q2. Do you think the size of the font is too small?
> Answers: yes: 42 no: 15

4) a) What is a <u>design specification</u>?
   b) List some things that a design specification should include.
   c) Write a design specification for a <u>display stand</u> for a new chocolate bar.

Development and Evaluation

There's only so much <u>development</u> you can do <u>on paper</u>. Making <u>mock-ups</u>, <u>models</u> and <u>prototypes</u> of your product means that you can <u>test</u>, <u>evaluate</u> and <u>modify</u> the design.

Different Sorts of Model are Used at Different Stages

Models can be <u>2D or 3D drawings</u> done by hand or using CAD (see page 62).
In 3D CAD packages you can view a <u>virtual reality</u> model from <u>all angles</u>. Or you could actually <u>make</u> 3D models, maybe <u>scaled down</u> in size, to check the shape of the design.

Mock-ups are usually <u>full scale</u> and made of <u>cheap</u> paper and card.
A full scale mock-up will help you check that your design is <u>ergonomic</u>.
You might also use a mock-up to quickly check the construction of <u>nets</u>,
or for a <u>magazine</u> or <u>menu</u> design to check the colours and images.

Not that kind...

Mock-ups are called prototypes if they're a full scale <u>working product</u>.
Prototypes include all the <u>components</u> and <u>mechanisms</u>, and they're
made using the right <u>materials</u> and <u>construction</u> methods.

See below for more on prototypes.

Models and Mock-Ups are Used to Improve the Design

Making models and mock-ups is a good way to spot and solve <u>problems</u>.

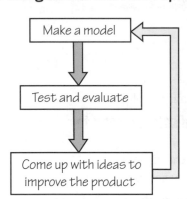

Make a model → Test and evaluate → Come up with ideas to improve the product

1) You can make models using materials that are <u>easy</u> and <u>quick</u> to work with, e.g. <u>cardboard</u>, <u>balsa wood</u> or <u>expanded polystyrene</u>.

2) After you've made each model, do some <u>tests</u> (see next page) to check that it works how it's supposed to.

3) You should also <u>evaluate</u> each model against the <u>design specification</u>. Take each point and see if your model is up to scratch.

4) There are probably some things that <u>don't work out</u> quite how you'd hoped. <u>Write down</u> what the problem is, suggest how to <u>fix it</u> and make another model.

5) Record how the design develops — <u>take photos</u> of your models.

Prototypes Help Manufacturers Avoid Big Mistakes

A lot of <u>money</u> is at stake when new products are introduced. Making a <u>prototype</u> before the final <u>industrial production</u> helps ensure that money isn't <u>wasted</u>.

1) You can <u>test</u> that the product <u>works</u> properly and is <u>safe</u>.

2) You can ask potential <u>end-users</u> (customers) for <u>feedback</u>, to see whether the product <u>meets their needs</u>.

3) If the prototype <u>works well</u> and potential customers <u>like it</u>, a manufacturer would consider going into production on a <u>larger scale</u>.

The final product you make for your controlled assessment is a <u>prototype</u>. You'll have to do a <u>final evaluation</u> of it, covering this stuff and saying whether it meets the specification.

A good model — serious expression, striking a pose...

Models are really important in design. It'd be a bad, bad, bad idea to go straight from the 2D drawings to making the final product — a lot of potential problems are ironed out during the modelling stage.

Development and Evaluation

Testing can be Destructive or Non-destructive

Products can be <u>tested</u> in different ways:

1) <u>Non-destructive testing</u> doesn't damage the product — it tests it doing its <u>normal job</u> to see <u>how well it works</u> and to make sure it <u>doesn't break</u>. For example, you might test whether a paper cup <u>holds water</u>.

2) Some testing is <u>physical</u> and <u>destroys</u> the product to see <u>when</u> and <u>how</u> it fails. This is <u>destructive testing</u>. It helps manufacturers to write <u>instructions</u> for their products — e.g. <u>packaging</u> might be labelled with <u>maximum loads</u>.

Sarah tests her book to make sure the spine doesn't break.

Consult Other People About Your Design

1) Find out people's opinions about your various <u>models</u>.

2) This will help you <u>refine</u> your ideas so you can arrive at the best solution.

3) Relevant <u>market research</u> questions might include:

- Do you find the text easy to read?
- Do you like the colours?
- What is the most striking feature?
- What don't you like about the product?
- How much would you be willing to pay?

So would you consider buying one?

Practice Questions

1) Laura wants to make a <u>scaled down 3D model</u> of her design for a clock.
   a) Suggest why Laura wants to make this type of model.
   b) Suggest some <u>materials</u> she could use for the model.
   c) What should Laura use the model for?

2) What is the difference between a <u>mock-up</u> and a <u>prototype</u>?

3) Doris has designed some weighing scales. She has made a <u>prototype</u> of her design. Describe how Doris could use the prototype to help her decide whether to go into <u>larger scale</u> production.

4) a) What is <u>non-destructive</u> testing?
   b) Why is <u>destructive testing</u> useful?

5) Zara has made mock-ups of some <u>pop-up birthday cards</u>. She plans to do some market research. Suggest four <u>market research questions</u> she could ask about her mock-up cards.

Manufacturing Specification

In industry, designers usually just <u>design</u> things — they don't make them as well.
So they have to tell the <u>manufacturer</u> exactly <u>what</u> the product is and <u>how</u> to make it.

You Need to Produce a Manufacturing Specification

A manufacturing specification can be a <u>series of written statements</u>, or <u>working drawings</u> and <u>sequence diagrams</u> (see next page). It has to explain <u>exactly</u> how to make the product, and should include:

1) <u>clear construction details</u> explaining <u>exactly</u> how to make each part,

2) <u>materials</u> — which materials to use for each part and how much will be needed,

3) <u>sizes</u> — <u>precise measurements</u> of each part in <u>millimetres</u>,

4) <u>tolerances</u> — the maximum and minimum sizes each part should be,

5) <u>finishing</u> details — any special information, such as 'laminate the paper with aluminium',

6) <u>quality control</u> instructions — what needs to be checked, and how and when to check it.

7) <u>costings</u> — how much each part costs, and details of any other costs involved.

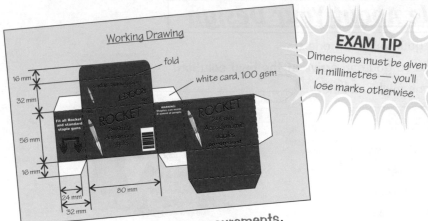

Working Drawing

fold

white card, 100 gsm

16 mm
32 mm
56 mm
16 mm
24 mm
32 mm
80 mm

Fit all Rocket and standard staple guns

ROCKET

Working drawings give <u>measurements</u>, <u>materials</u> and <u>construction</u> details (e.g. where to make folds).

EXAM TIP
Dimensions must be given in millimetres — you'll lose marks otherwise.

<u>Spreadsheets</u> are great for working out <u>costings</u>.

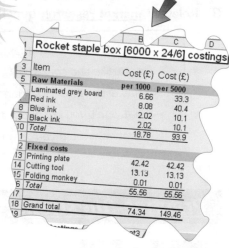

Rocket staple box [6000 x 24/6] costings

	B	C	D
Item		Cost (£)	Cost (£)
Raw Materials		per 1000	per 5000
Laminated grey board			
Red ink		6.66	33.3
Blue ink		8.08	40.4
Black ink		2.02	10.1
Total		2.02	10.1
		18.78	93.9
Fixed costs			
Printing plate			
Cutting tool		42.42	42.42
Folding monkey		13.13	13.13
Total		0.01	0.01
		55.56	55.56
Grand total		74.34	149.46

Plan Each Stage in Detail

Take <u>each stage</u> of the process and plan it <u>in detail</u>. You need to think about:

1) <u>how long</u> each stage will take,

2) what needs to be <u>prepared</u> before you can start each stage,

3) how you will <u>ensure consistency</u> and <u>quality</u>, e.g. using <u>jigs</u>, <u>formers</u> and <u>measuring tools</u>,

4) how you will do <u>quality control checks</u>,

5) what <u>health and safety precautions</u> you will have to take to be safe when making your product.

Remember, your <u>methods</u> would probably <u>change</u> if you were going to produce your design in <u>quantity</u>. (In your project, you should definitely write about <u>how</u> they'd change.)

Clear construction details — "Insert tab A into slot B..."*

If you don't plan carefully, something's bound to go wrong and you'll have to <u>waste time</u> putting it right. Planning's vital in <u>industry</u> too — because <u>time is money</u>. (Wasting loads of <u>materials</u> isn't great either.)

* ...which doesn't fit, so try it in every other slot before widening slot B until it does actually fit. Repeat for tabs B, C and D.

Manufacturing Specification

Making a few examples of your product is (relatively) easy. But mass-producing it is a whole different ball game. And it takes a shed-load of careful planning.

(You can of course plan things <u>in a shed</u>, while <u>bouncing a ball</u> against the wall.)

Use Charts to Help You

You need to work out <u>what order</u> to do things in.

① **Work Order** This can be produced as a <u>table</u> or <u>flow chart</u>. The purpose of a work order is to plan the <u>sequence</u> in which tasks should be carried out. The plan could include tools, quality control stages, safety, and so on.

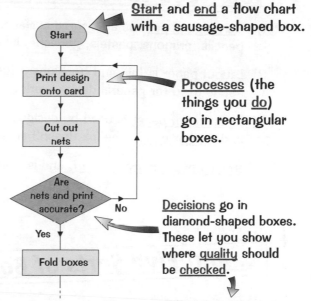

<u>Start</u> and <u>end</u> a flow chart with a sausage-shaped box.

Processes (the things you <u>do</u>) go in rectangular boxes.

<u>Decisions</u> go in diamond-shaped boxes. These let you show where <u>quality</u> should be <u>checked</u>.

Prototype staple box			
Day	Process	Tools needed	Quality ch
1	Print designs	Airbrush, pens, dry transfer lettering	Make s
2	Cut out net	Scalpel, metal rule	Chec
	Score and fold net	Scissors, metal rule	

The diamond shaped boxes show where you will stop and see if your product looks and works how it should. If you find it doesn't, go back and make sure it's done properly before you move on.

You also need to work out <u>how long</u> each stage will take, and how these times will fit into the <u>total time</u> you've allowed for production. One way to do this is with a Gantt chart:

② **Gantt Chart** The tasks are listed down the <u>left-hand</u> side, and the <u>timing</u> is plotted across the top. The coloured squares show <u>how long</u> each task takes and the <u>order</u> they're done in.

	5 mins	10 mins	15 mins	20 mins	25 mins	30 mins	35 mins	40 mins	45 mins	50 mins	55 mins	60 mins	65 mins	70 mins	75 mins	80 mins	85 mins	90 mins	95 mins	100 mins
Mark out box and cutting template																				
Mask white areas, airbrush box																				
Allow paint to dry																				
Cut out cutting template																				
Apply writing																				
Outline logo with fine marker																				
Colour logo with paint or felt tips																				
Use template to cut box out																				
Mark out and score folds																				
Assemble box																				

You can start the next stage while the paint's drying, so draw the bars underneath each other.

Practice Questions

1) a) What is a <u>manufacturing specification</u>?
   b) List <u>three things</u> that a manufacturing specification might include.

2) What are <u>working drawings</u>?

3) On a flow chart, how would you show where <u>quality control</u> should take place?

4) Mike is making an <u>orange juice carton</u>. He has made a Gantt chart of the process.
   a) Why don't any of the bars <u>overlap</u>?
   b) How long does the <u>whole process</u> last?
   c) Which is the <u>longest stage</u>? How long does it last?

	5 mins	10 mins	15 mins	20 mins	25 mins	30 mins	35 mins	40 mins	45 mins	50 mins	55 mins	60 mins	65 mins	70 mins	75 mins	80 mins
Laminate paper with aluminium																
Cut out shape of carton																
Mask white areas, airbrush carton																
Allow paint to dry																
Apply writing and logo																
Mark and score folds																
Assemble carton																

Section 1 — The Design Process

Paper and Board

There are lots of sorts of <u>paper</u> and <u>board</u> — each designed for a particular use. Paper and board are pretty useful for <u>writing</u> and <u>sketching</u> (no, really) and also for making products like <u>packaging</u>.

You Need to Know About Four Sorts of Paper...

1) <u>Cartridge paper</u> has a <u>textured</u> surface, which is great for sketching with pencils, crayons, pastels, gouache, inks and watercolours.

2) <u>Layout paper</u> is <u>thin</u> and <u>translucent</u> (you can see light through it) and is used for general design work — particularly sketching ideas.

3) <u>Bleed-proof paper</u> is used by designers when drawing with <u>felt-tips</u> and <u>marker pens</u>. The ink doesn't spread out (<u>bleed</u>) — it stays put.

4) <u>Tracing paper</u> is <u>translucent</u>, and is used to <u>copy images</u>.

Ink bleeds on some paper because the paper fibres suck the ink away.

...and Five Sorts of Board

The weight of paper and board is measured in <u>gsm</u> (grams per square metre). Above <u>200 gsm</u>, it's not paper any more — it's <u>board</u>. Sometimes you're given the <u>thickness</u> instead, in <u>microns</u> (one micron is one thousandth of a millimetre).

1) <u>Solid white board</u> has a high quality bleached surface, which is ideal for printing. It's used loads for <u>primary packaging</u> — packaging for individual items. (<u>Secondary packaging</u> is used to contain lots of the same item — see below.)

2) <u>Mount board</u> is used to mount drawings and photographs for presentation or framing — usually by cutting a 'window' into the board.

3) <u>Corrugated board</u> is used a lot in <u>secondary</u> packaging to protect products during transit. It's made up of a <u>fluted inner oore</u> sandwiched between <u>two outer layers</u>.

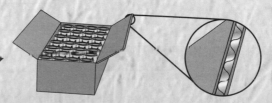

4) <u>Duplex board</u> has a <u>different colour</u> and <u>texture</u> on <u>each side</u>. It's often used where only <u>one surface</u> is <u>seen</u>, so that only one side needs to be <u>smooth</u> for <u>printing</u>. It's <u>unbleached</u>, so it's ideal for food packaging.

5) <u>Grey board</u> is rigid. It's easy to <u>cover with paper</u> so that <u>graphics</u> can be printed onto it. It's found in game boards, hardback books, ring binders, and covered boxes.

I'm board — are we nearly there yet...

All these different types of paper and board are here for a reason — each one's best at a different job. Learn their properties in case you get asked which sort you should use in your exam *paper*... (Geddit?)

Paper and Board

Board is Often Made from Recycled Paper

1) <u>Paper</u> and <u>board</u> are made from <u>wood pulp</u>. If the pulp comes from <u>well-managed forests</u>, paper and board are fairly <u>sustainable materials</u>.

2) Most types of paper and board are <u>recyclable</u>. Lots of <u>cardboard</u> is made from recycled material — making it even more <u>environmentally friendly</u>.

3) '<u>Virgin</u>' paper is made from <u>new wood pulp</u>, <u>not recycled</u> material.

4) Paper and board are <u>biodegradable</u> — they'll <u>rot away</u> naturally (quite quickly if you <u>shred</u> them).

You Can Buy Paper in Standard Sizes

1) Paper sizes go <u>from A0</u> (which has an area of 1 m²) to <u>A1</u>, <u>A2</u>, and so on — halving in size (area) each time.

2) Many other sizes are also available:
   - <u>A4</u> paper is <u>half</u> the size of <u>A3</u> paper.
   - <u>A5</u> paper is <u>half</u> the size of <u>A4</u> paper.
   - <u>A6</u> paper is <u>half</u> the size of <u>A5</u> paper.

   As the paper gets smaller the number increases.

   > The width of A3 paper is the length of A4.
   > The length of A3 paper is double the width of A4.

3) The most common paper sizes used in schools are <u>A4</u> and <u>A3</u>.
   A4 is 297 mm × 210 mm, in case you're interested.

Clever Ben has correctly labelled these sheets of paper. Well done, Ben!

Practice Questions

1) What type of paper is often used for drawing with <u>felt-tip</u> and <u>marker pens</u>? Explain why.

2) a) What's the surface of <u>cartridge paper</u> like?
   b) What would you use it for?

3) What properties do <u>layout paper</u> and <u>tracing paper</u> have in common?

4) In what <u>units</u> are the weights of paper and card measured?

5) Describe <u>duplex board</u>, and say why it's used a lot in food packaging.

6) a) What's the difference between <u>primary</u> and <u>secondary</u> packaging?
   b) What type of board might you use for each?

7) Laura wants to make a sturdy ring-binder with pictures and text <u>printed</u> on the outside. What type of board would be best and why?

8) Explain why <u>cardboard</u> is quite an <u>environmentally friendly</u> product.

9) What <u>standard size</u> is this piece of yellow paper?

Paper and Board

Laminating means <u>adding a layer</u> of something <u>different</u>, like spreading jam onto your toast.

Paper Can be Laminated...

If you <u>laminate</u> paper by adding a <u>layer</u> of <u>another material</u>, you get a <u>composite</u> with <u>different qualities</u>. For example...

A composite is made up of two or more different materials.

Ernie misunderstood his boss's instruction to build a laminator.

ALUMINIUM

A combination of paper and <u>aluminium foil</u> is used to <u>package food</u>.

This keeps <u>flavours in</u> and <u>air out</u>, and you can print <u>graphics</u> onto the paper.

POLYTHENE

Paper can be coated with <u>polythene</u> to make it <u>waterproof</u>.

Then you can use it for things like <u>paper cups</u>, where normal paper would go soggy pretty quickly.

Second time round, the laminator was more successful — but still not quite right.

POLYSTYRENE

<u>Foam core board</u> is made by laminating polystyrene foam between card.

It's <u>stiff</u> but <u>lightweight</u>, and is used for mounting posters and making models.

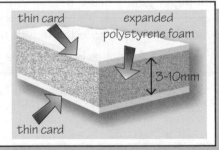

thin card

expanded polystyrene foam

3-10mm

thin card

...And Made Into Spiral Wound Tubes...

1) <u>Spiral wound tubes</u> are made from paper wound in a spiral (no kidding) and held together with <u>glue</u>. They're <u>light</u> but the tube shape makes them <u>strong</u>.

2) They're often given a nice <u>finish</u> — the tube is covered with a single sheet of paper that's smooth and easy to print on.

3) They're made in all sorts of sizes — e.g. for use in fireworks, toilet rolls and snack containers.

Remember the finish — they have lovely lakes, trees, saunas...

As soon as you think you've learnt the properties of paper and board, they go and invent a new load by bunging some other material onto it. Guess what — you've got to learn these ones too, I'm afraid.

Paper and Board

How to Pick the Right Paper and Board

Different sorts of paper and board have pros and cons — you need to be ready to weigh them up.

COST AND QUALITY

If you use expensive paper and board, it makes your item feel high quality. It also adds to the final price of the product — so it's only worth doing for luxury products, or products that have to last a long time, like certificates.

FLEXIBILITY AND RIGIDITY

To make 3D products, you need paper and board that can be bent or folded without breaking but is rigid enough to keep its shape (if it's used as a box, say). Corrugated board is a good option when you need quite a strong, stiff material.

FINISH

Solid white board has an excellent surface for printing on, but you can save money by using cheaper recycled board laminated with high quality paper, e.g. for toy packaging. For something that doesn't need a good finish (if it'll end up hidden, say), you could just use plain recycled board.

STRENGTH AND WEIGHT

Some materials, such as corrugated cardboard or grey board, can withstand a fair bit of force without breaking — so they're good for heavy-duty packaging or making products that will be handled a lot, e.g. box files. Stronger materials are usually heavier or bulkier though — this adds to transport costs (and the extra fuel burned is bad for the environment).

ENVIRONMENT AND SUSTAINABILITY

Using recycled materials preserves woodlands and saves energy that would have been used to pulp new wood. However, recycled paper and board may contain toxic chemicals that mean they're not suitable for packaging food. Laminated paper can be hard to recycle, because it's difficult to separate the paper from the other materials.

Margot always enjoyed weighing up the pros and cons of different types of paper.

Practice Questions

1) Describe the structure of foam core board. Suggest what you'd use it for.

2) Delia has invented a new mustard, sherry and cheese sauce. She wants to package it in a paper carton.
   a) Suggest what material the paper should be laminated with.
   b) How would using this material change the properties of the carton?
   c) Suggest a possible environmental problem of using this composite material.

3) a) What are spiral wound tubes made from?
   b) What properties do they have?

4) What are the benefits and drawbacks of using thick board instead of thin card for packaging?

5) List some factors you should think about when choosing which paper or board to use.

Plastics

There are two main types of plastic — thermosetting and thermoplastics. Luckily, you only need to know about <u>thermoplastics</u>. These are moulded by heating and can be <u>re-moulded</u> if you heat them again.

There are Many Different Thermoplastics

1) <u>Acetate</u> (<u>cellulose acetate</u>) is <u>flexible</u>, <u>hard</u>, <u>shiny</u> and <u>transparent</u> (see-through) or <u>translucent</u> (lets light through). It's used in <u>thin sheets</u> for overhead projector transparencies, and for packaging where the product needs to be <u>seen</u>. It's easy to print on. It's made mostly from wood so it's a bit more <u>sustainable</u> than many plastics.

2) <u>Polypropylene</u> (<u>PP</u>) is <u>quite strong</u>, <u>tough</u> and <u>flexible</u>. Products can be made with a '<u>living hinge</u>' (box, lid and hinge all made out of one piece of polypropylene) — which is handy for lunch boxes, etc. It's also used for <u>packaging</u>, <u>chairs</u>, <u>textiles</u> and <u>car parts</u>.

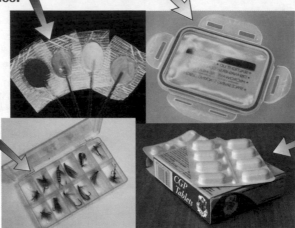

3) <u>High Impact Polystyrene</u> (<u>HIPS</u>) is rigid and comes in a variety of colours and thicknesses. It's used for making <u>boxes</u> for products and for <u>vacuum forming</u>. It's fairly <u>cheap</u>.

4) <u>Polyvinyl chloride</u> (<u>PVC</u>) is <u>cheap</u> and <u>durable</u>, easy to <u>print</u> on, but quite <u>brittle</u>. It's used for <u>blister packs</u> (e.g. for holding pills or screws), <u>vinyl records</u>, <u>insulation</u> for electrical wires, etc.

Plastics Can be Used for Modelling

The following plastic materials aren't very strong but they're <u>easy to cut and shape</u>. That makes them useful as <u>modelling materials</u> — for seeing your ideas in <u>3D</u>:

1) <u>Corrugated plastic sheet</u> is <u>lightweight</u>, <u>rigid</u> and <u>weatherproof</u>. It's made from polypropylene. Although it's fairly stiff it can still be <u>bent into shapes</u>, so it's good for modelling objects with large <u>flat surfaces</u> and <u>square edges</u> — e.g. the outside cases of electronic items. It's also often used for estate agents' sign boards and students' folders.

2) <u>Expanded polystyrene foam</u> is a <u>lightweight</u> material that you can shape with a <u>knife</u> or more accurately with a <u>hot-wire cutter</u>. Some types are quite <u>crumbly</u> (these types are often used as protective packaging). Other types have a fairly <u>dense structure</u>, e.g. <u>STYROFOAM</u>™ (which is usually <u>blue</u>). Expanded polystyrene foam is good for making 3D models but you need to <u>fill</u> the surface (see page 22) if you're going to paint the model.

3) <u>Machining foam</u> is much more <u>compact</u> than expanded polystyrene, so you can work on it with <u>machine tools</u> without it crumbling. You can make <u>detailed</u> pieces that can be <u>painted</u> — it's used to make architectural models, for example.

The month before your exams — it's the vinyl countdown...

OK, so revising plastics is about as much fun as trainspotting while someone slaps you with a haddock. Still, it's worth it when you sit down in an exam and read a question that you can answer straight away.

Plastics

Choose the Right Plastic for the Job

Designers need to select the best material to fit a <u>particular brief</u> — working through
a <u>specification</u> will let you <u>rule out</u> some plastics and pick the <u>best</u> of the rest.

<u>For example</u>: choose a plastic for a <u>signboard</u> to show the name of an election candidate:

SPECIFICATION

Must come in sheets <u>rigid</u> enough to
withstand <u>windy weather</u>.

Should be <u>cheap</u> rather than <u>high quality</u>
or <u>strong</u> — doesn't need to <u>last long</u>
or <u>bear weight</u>.

Finish — must be <u>coloured</u> and
easy to <u>print on</u>.

Would help to be <u>lightweight</u> —
will need to be <u>transported</u>.

Would help to be <u>recyclable</u> —
only has a <u>short lifespan</u>.

FLEXIBILITY, RIGIDITY AND STRENGTH

<u>Acetate</u> sheets would
be no good — they're
not rigid enough.

FINISH

<u>Acetate</u>, <u>PVC</u> and
<u>corrugated plastic</u>
can all be <u>printed on</u>.
However, <u>acetate</u> is
<u>see-through</u>.

COST AND QUALITY

Polypropylene is <u>strong</u>
and <u>tough</u> enough, but
the sign doesn't need
to be high quality so
<u>cheaper materials</u> will
do the job just as well.

WEIGHT

A sheet of rigid <u>PVC</u>
wouldn't need to be very
thick, so it'd be <u>light</u>.
However, corrugated
plastic is <u>even lighter</u>.

SUSTAINABILITY

Most plastics are made from <u>crude oil</u>, which will eventually all
be <u>used up</u> — so they're not very sustainable. Some plastics
can be <u>recycled</u>, and each type has an identifying mark for
recycling. Lots of <u>polypropylene</u> is recycled, but not much
<u>PVC</u> is. Most plastic waste still ends up in <u>landfill sites</u> — it
doesn't rot away naturally so can't be composted.

Left to right:
Polyvinyl chloride,
Polypropylene,
Polystyrene,
Pollywantsacracker.

DECISION

<u>Corrugated plastic</u> seems to be the ideal material.
It fits each part of the specification pretty well.

Practice Questions

1) What are the two main types of <u>polystyrene</u>? Outline their properties.

2) Hugh wants to <u>print</u> onto a plastic product. Which plastics are easy to print on?

3) Steve wants to make <u>models</u> of his ideas for a new computer casing.
   Which plastic modelling material would be easiest to use for modelling a design that has:
   a) square corners and flat sides?
   b) smooth, rounded corners and curved sides?

4) Rick has designed a card game. He's thinking about how best to <u>package</u> it.
   What plastic would be best to use if he wanted to sell the pack of cards:
   a) wrapped in a see-through plastic packet?
   b) mounted in a card-backed blister pack?

5) Explain why most plastics aren't <u>sustainable</u>.

Modern and Smart Materials

Smart materials and new modern materials are being developed all the time.
They allow new products to be made and problems with current products to be solved.

Some Modern Materials are Good for the Environment

1) Cornstarch polymers, potatopak and paper foam are all made from plants.

2) They're renewable materials — you can always grow some more plants.

3) They're biodegradable — when you've finished with them they'll rot away in a compost heap.

4) They're sometimes used as a more sustainable alternative to plastics —
   this saves finite resources like oil, and creates less need for landfill waste.

CORNSTARCH POLYMERS

- Are made from maize (sweetcorn).
- Can be made in a clear, flexible form for sandwich packaging, disposable cups, etc.
- They're also used for compostable bags.

EXAM TIP
These materials will come in handy if you're asked to choose one with minimal environmental impacts.

POTATOPAK

- Is made of dried potato starch that is baked inside moulds.
- It's fairly rigid and lightweight.
- It's good for making plates, trays, and packaging for food.

PAPER FOAM

- Is a composite of potato starch and paper fibres.
- It's lightweight and printable.
- It can be used in CD, DVD and mobile phone packaging.

Tracklisting
1. Paper foam
2. Paper foam
3. Paper foam
4. Paper foam
5. Paper foam

Precious Metal Clay is Used to Make Jewellery

Precious Metal Clay is a new material that contains particles of metal (often silver) in a binding material. It's often used to make jewellery.

The clay is really easy to work with — you can cut it, roll it and shape it like modelling clay.

When the clay is heated, the binder burns away, and the metal fuses together to create a solid metal object.

After it's heated, you can solder and polish it too.

Smart and modern — like all good celebrities...

These materials aren't just smart, they're devious. It'll start out as an innocent question about teacups and then BAM! you'll be asked how to make them change colour in response to heat. So watch out.

Modern and Smart Materials

Smart Materials React to Their Environment

1) Smart materials <u>change</u> their <u>properties</u> in response to <u>heat</u>, <u>light</u>, <u>pressure</u> or something else (depending on the material).

2) They often <u>change back</u> to their <u>original state</u> when the heat or light (or whatever else affects them) is <u>taken away</u>.

3) Some smart materials can let you make totally <u>new products</u>.

Thermochromic Materials

These <u>change colour</u> with <u>heat</u> (they go back to their original colour when they cool down).

Blue spoon...   ...gets hot...   ...and becomes pink.

With her thermochromic spoon, Goldilocks was the terror of the local bear population.

- Thermochromic <u>paints</u> can be used to create <u>images</u> that <u>change</u>, e.g. on mugs when hot water is poured in.

- Thermochromic <u>inks</u> can be used for <u>warning patches</u> that tell you if something is <u>too hot</u> (e.g. on <u>computer chips</u> or <u>feeding spoons</u> for babies). Ink on the patch changes colour as the product gets hotter. They can be <u>cheaper</u> and <u>more reliable</u> than electronic heat warnings.

Practice Questions

1) Waitburys supermarket want to replace the plastics used in some of their packaging with more <u>environmentally friendly</u> materials. What material would you suggest for:
   a) transparent boxes for cream cakes?
   b) trays of sweetcorn?
   c) protective inserts for a digital camera box?

2) A supermarket chain claims that they package most of their food with <u>potatopak</u>. Describe the potential <u>environmental benefits</u> of using potatopak.

3) Jess has a ring made from <u>PMC</u>.
   a) What does PMC stand for?
   b) Outline how the ring would have been made.

4) Paul is designing a label for his Dandelion and Burdock drink bottle. The drink should be served <u>chilled</u> and he wants the label to show when the drink is <u>cool enough</u>. Paul's teacher tells him he could use a <u>smart material</u> to do this.
   a) What is a smart material?
   b) Suggest which smart material he could use, and describe how it would work.

Fillers and Finishing

Finishes are applied to a model or product to <u>protect</u> it from <u>damage</u> and <u>dirt</u> and to improve its <u>appearance</u>. But before being painted or varnished, some surfaces need <u>filling and sanding</u>...

Fillers Prepare Surfaces for Finishing

Your product won't look very good if the surface is horribly <u>holey</u> or <u>cracked</u>. And you <u>can't</u> just fill in the cracks with paint — you need <u>fillers</u>.

1) <u>Plaster filler</u> is a powder that you mix with water into a thick paste. It can <u>fill small cracks</u> and <u>improve the surface finish</u> of <u>foam models</u>.

2) If you're using <u>balsa wood</u>, <u>plywood</u> or <u>MDF</u> in your model, you'd be better off using <u>wood filler</u>.

Mark decided the best thing to fill his crackers with was cheese.

You need to Prepare the Surface Before Applying Filler

Check that the filler is <u>suitable</u> for the <u>material</u> — and always try it on a small <u>sample</u> piece first.

①First you need to <u>lightly rub down</u> the surface using sandpaper to give a <u>rough surface</u> for the filler to stick to — this is called <u>keying</u>.

②Make sure the surface is <u>clean</u> — <u>wipe</u> all the dust off.

③Apply the filler to areas where it's needed and <u>leave to dry</u> until it's <u>hard</u>.

④Sand the filler back to a <u>smooth</u> flat surface using rough then smooth sandpaper.

EXAM TIP
If you're asked how to apply a filler, don't forget to talk about <u>surface preparation</u> first.

You may need to <u>repeat this process</u> a number of times to get a really <u>smooth surface</u>.

Paints and Varnishes can be Used to Finish Surfaces...

Once you've prepared and filled the surface, you can apply paint or varnish.

PAINTS

1) These are made up of a <u>pigment</u> (a colour) and a <u>vehicle</u> (a solvent that <u>carries</u> the pigment).
2) There's a whole load of different vehicles — e.g. <u>water</u>, <u>acrylic</u>, <u>cellulose</u>, <u>oil</u>, etc.
3) Once the paint has been applied, the vehicle <u>evaporates</u> to leave just the pigment.
4) Water based and acrylic paints take <u>less time</u> to <u>dry</u> than oil paints.

SPIRIT VARNISH/LACQUERS

1) These consist of a <u>synthetic (man-made) resin</u> (e.g. acrylic resin, cellulose resin) dissolved in an <u>organic solvent</u>.
2) The solvent <u>evaporates</u> to leave a thin <u>protective layer</u> of transparent varnish.
3) Using an <u>ultra violet (UV)</u> varnish on paper products gives a glossy, <u>professional-looking</u> finish and makes the paper more <u>durable</u>.

See page 75 for more on varnishing.

Builders use fillers for some of their visible cracks...

<u>Preparing the surface</u> properly before painting or varnishing really is the secret of success. After all, you wouldn't expect to pass an exam with <u>flying colours</u> unless you'd <u>prepared</u> for it by <u>learning your stuff</u>.

Fillers and Finishing

...But Some Surfaces Need to be Primed First

Not all <u>varnishes</u> and <u>paints</u> stick well to all <u>materials</u> — so try your finish on a sample of the material first.

① Clean the surface

② Prime the surface

Some materials need a <u>primer</u> — this is a first coat that <u>seals</u> the surface of the material and gives the finish something to <u>stick</u> to.

③ Choose how to apply the finish...

<u>Brushes</u> come in different shapes and sizes — so you can apply paint <u>accurately</u>.

<u>Spray cans</u> give <u>quick</u> and <u>even</u> coverage, but you'll need to <u>mask</u> areas that you don't want to paint.

<u>Rollers</u> are <u>quick</u> and <u>easy</u> to use and you don't get brush marks.

④ Apply the finish

You should apply the finish in several <u>thin</u> coats. Each coat will dry quickly and be <u>less likely</u> to have <u>drips</u> and <u>streaks</u> in.

⑤ Smooth the finish

Use <u>fine sandpaper</u> to smooth <u>each coat</u> when it's dried — then wipe the <u>dust</u> off with a clean cloth before applying the next coat.

Remember to <u>clean your brushes</u> when you've finished painting or varnishing, using <u>water</u> for water-based finishes and <u>white spirit</u> for oil-based ones. (Check the instructions on the tin — they usually tell you what to use.)

You Can Laminate Paper or Card

<u>Laminating</u> (or <u>encapsulation</u>) is a quick and effective way to finish a piece of work on paper or thin card. Laminating uses heat to <u>sandwich</u> the paper or card between <u>two layers of plastic</u> (see page 41). This gives a professional finish to posters, menus, bookmarks, etc.

Practice Questions

1) Suggest what you could use to fill some small cracks in a piece of <u>machining foam</u>.

2) Describe the four stages in applying a <u>filler</u>.

3) Terry wants to <u>paint</u> his balsa wood prototype of his design for a <u>mobile phone</u>. Suggest:
   a) what he should do to the prototype to <u>prepare</u> it for finishing.
   b) what he should use to <u>apply</u> the finish.
   c) why he should apply the finish in <u>several layers</u>.

4) Cuthbert wants to make <u>menus</u> to stand on the tables of his new restaurant. Suggest a technique he could use to give the menus a <u>professional-looking finish</u>.

Drawing and Painting

When you're making <u>presentation drawings</u> there are <u>loads of different media</u> to choose from.

Pencils are Ace
"You can lead a horse to water but a pencil must be lead." (Stan Laurel)

1) Pencils are made from a mixture of <u>graphite</u> (a form of carbon) and clay.

2) They are classified by their <u>hardness</u> (<u>H</u>) and <u>blackness</u> (<u>B</u>) and range from <u>9H</u> (least graphite) to <u>9B</u> (most graphite).

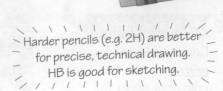

hardest																		blackest
9H	8H	7H	6H	5H	4H	3H	2H	H	HB	B	2B	3B	4B	5B	6B	7B	8B	9B

more graphite — softer

3) <u>Coloured pencils</u> come in a variety of hardnesses — the softer ones produce an <u>even</u>, <u>flat</u> colour.

Harder pencils (e.g. 2H) are better for precise, technical drawing. HB is good for sketching.

Inks, Paints, Pastels, Dry-Transfer Lettering... also Ace

INKS
These are pigments suspended in water or another solvent. They're good for <u>colour infilling</u>, <u>background washes</u> and <u>writing</u>.

CHALK PASTELS
You can use chalk pastel for <u>backgrounds</u> or to add <u>tone and shading</u>. It's easily <u>blended</u> using your fingers or cotton wool.

GOUACHE
<u>Gouache</u> is an <u>opaque paint</u> (not see-through). You can use it for <u>flat areas of colour</u> or for adding <u>highlights</u>.

DRY-TRANSFER LETTERING
This is applied with <u>pressure</u> from a <u>waxed</u> translucent sheet onto <u>drawings</u> or <u>3D prototypes</u>.

Airbrushes Blow a Mist of Ink

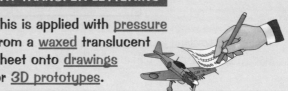
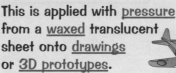

← air

1) Airbrushes blow a <u>fine mist of ink</u> from a reservoir using <u>compressed air</u>.

2) You have to <u>mask</u> all the areas you don't want to airbrush. Use low-tack clear film — and cut it with a craft knife so you get clean edges.

Felt Pens and Markers Dry Quickly

1) <u>Fine-liners</u> come in a variety of thicknesses and colours. They're <u>great</u> for drawing fine, precise lines and <u>outlining drawings</u>, e.g. orthographic drawings.

2) <u>Markers</u> are available in hundreds of different colour tones. They're great for thicker lines. You can get markers with different tips (<u>chisel</u>, <u>bullet</u> and <u>brush</u>).

Let's draw this page to a close now — I'm in a brush...

Computer packages, e.g. <u>Adobe® Photoshop®</u>, can be used to create effects that look like they've been done by hand — they can produce graphics that look like they've been <u>airbrushed</u> or <u>shaded with chalk</u>.

Drawing and Painting

Drawing Boards can Make Drawing Easier

1) You can use a piece of <u>blockboard</u> or <u>plywood</u> as a basic <u>drawing board</u>.

2) <u>Free-standing</u> ones are more expensive and include a mechanism to adjust the angle of the board — and some have an integrated <u>parallel motion</u> or <u>T-square</u> for drawing horizontal and vertical lines.

Drawing Apparatus Increases Accuracy and Precision

Set Squares, Rulers and Protractors

1) <u>Set squares</u> are used for <u>drawing</u> and <u>checking angles</u>.

2) You use a <u>30-60-90°</u> set square for <u>isometric</u> projection (see page 43).

3) A <u>45-45-90°</u> set square is used for <u>orthographic</u> projections.

4) Hopefully you know what <u>rulers</u> are for. Examiners <u>hate wiggly lines</u> that should be straight — so use a ruler.

5) <u>Protractors</u> are used to <u>measure</u> or <u>draw angles</u>.

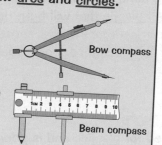

EXAM TIP
<u>Clean</u> your set squares and ruler or you'll <u>smudge</u> things and the examiner won't be able to tell just how <u>perfect</u> your drawings are.

Curves and Templates

1) You can use <u>French curves</u> (or <u>ship's curves</u>) for drawing complex curves.

2) <u>Flexicurves</u> can be shaped into different profiles.

flexicurve

French curve template

3) You can use <u>ellipse</u> and <u>circle templates</u> to draw, errr, ellipses and circles.

4) <u>Eraser guides</u> protect a drawing while you're using an eraser. They make it easy to leave a highlight or tidy edge when erasing.

Compasses

1) You use these to draw <u>arcs</u> and <u>circles</u>.

2) <u>Bow compasses</u> are more accurate than those with an attached pencil.

3) <u>Beam compasses</u> are for larger drawings.

Bow compass

Beam compass

Practice Questions

1) What type of <u>pencil</u> would you use for:
   a) sketching several initial <u>design ideas</u>,
   b) <u>technical</u> drawing.

2) Chris wants to add <u>colour and shading</u> to his design drawings. Suggest what equipment would be suitable for this, and explain why.

3) What piece of <u>drawing apparatus</u> would you use to draw:
   a) a 60° angle,   b) a circle,   c) a curve.

4) Use a <u>protractor</u> to draw an angle measuring <u>50°</u>.

5) Use a pair of <u>compasses</u> to draw a circle with a <u>diameter</u> of 60 mm.

60 mm

Adhesives

There's an <u>adhesive</u> for almost <u>every</u> situation in life. Phew.

For Sticking Paper and Card...

1) You use `glue sticks` to bond paper and card. They're <u>non-toxic</u>, <u>cheap</u> and come in different sizes. Common brands include Pritt®, UHU® and Bostik. They're all clear when dry and are <u>environmentally friendly</u>.

2) You apply `rubber-based cement` (or <u>gum</u>) to <u>both surfaces</u> then leave it for about ten minutes before bringing the surfaces together. <u>Repositioning</u> is possible.

3) The glue in squeezy `glue pens` is <u>liquid</u> — so it can be <u>messy</u> to use. Glue pens bond paper and card and the glue is <u>clear</u> when dry.

4) You can use `aerosols` such as <u>SprayMount</u>™ and <u>PhotoMount</u>™ for mounting photos onto paper or card — they cover large areas well and allow for <u>repositioning</u> (unless it says 'permanent' on the tin...)

For Sticking Wood Together...

1) `Polyvinyl acetate (PVA)` glue is a <u>water-based</u> glue used to bond <u>wood</u>. It's also good for <u>paper</u> and <u>card</u> — though it takes a while to dry.

2) `Balsa cement` is good for sticking <u>balsa wood</u>. It's clear when dry.

3) You can use `glue guns` to quickly bond materials like <u>wood</u>, <u>fabric</u> and <u>card</u> together. They use a <u>low-melt plastic</u> that will <u>burn you</u> if it gets on your <u>skin</u>, so take <u>care</u>. The glue can leave gaps when it sets so don't use it for accurate prototypes or final products — but it's good for quick modelling.

For Sticking Acrylic...

`Acrylic cement` is also called <u>Tensol</u>®. It's used for <u>plastics</u> and is good for joints that won't be knocked. It gives off <u>harmful fumes</u> so you should only use it in a <u>well-ventilated</u> area.

For Sticking Most Materials...

1) You need to mix the two parts (<u>resin</u> and <u>hardener</u>) of `epoxy resin` glue (e.g. Araldite®). 'Rapid' versions set in about 5 minutes, so speed is essential.

2) You get `superglue` in small tubes — it quickly bonds a large variety of materials, e.g. ceramics, plastics, textiles and metal (and your fingers).

Chad fell for the old epoxy resin/hair gel switch-e-roo

Knock-Knock — 'Who's there?' — 'U' — 'U who?'...

There are loads of gives to stick things together — with more than one for each type of material. Try to figure out which one suits your needs the best. Don't get stuck in a rut — there's a glue for you.

Adhesives

There's also Sticky Tape...

Masking tape, Sellotape® and double-sided tape all come on <u>rolls</u>. They're not as good as <u>bacon</u> though.

Yup, you know what <u>Sellotape</u>® is for.

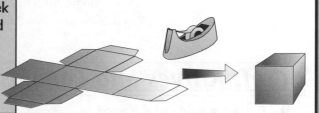

<u>Masking tape</u> is <u>low-tack</u> tape — it's easy to <u>remove</u>. You use it to stick paper to drawing boards or to <u>mask</u> areas when using pastels or markers.

<u>Double-sided tape</u> is often used to stick <u>card models</u> and <u>shape nets</u>. It's good if you want the join hidden from view. It's hard to remove once stuck down though — so make sure you put it in the right place first time.

...Sticky-Backed Plastic and Blu-Tack®

Adhesive plastic film

You use <u>adhesive plastic film</u> (also known as sticky-backed plastic) to <u>cover</u> and <u>protect</u> large, awkwardly shaped card and paper models when <u>laminating</u> them isn't possible.
Blue Peter eat your heart out.

Blu-Tack®

<u>Blu-Tack</u>® and white-tack are for <u>temporary fixing</u>. They're mainly used for sticking <u>posters to walls</u>, but also for <u>folder work</u> to allow for <u>repositioning</u>.

Practice Questions

1) What type of <u>glue</u> would you use to stick:
   a) two pieces of <u>paper</u> together?
   b) <u>photos</u> onto a piece of <u>card</u>?
   c) a piece of <u>paper</u> to a piece of <u>wood</u>?
   d) your <u>hands</u> together?

2) Sally is using a <u>glue gun</u> to stick some fabric to a wooden frame. Give one <u>precaution</u> she should take.

3) Outline how <u>epoxy resin</u> is used.

4) Derek is making a model of a house using <u>cardboard</u>.
   He needs to fold his shape net up to form the 3D model.
   a) Suggest how Derek could <u>secure</u> his shape net without affecting the outside of the model.
   b) Derek realises after he's made the 3D model that he needs to add a <u>protective covering</u> to it. Suggest what material he could use for this.

Tools

OK, you've probably known about scissors since you were old enough to run with them, but that's no excuse to skip these pages. There are plenty of other, more <u>exotic</u> cutting tools out there.

Good Old Scissors Cut Paper and Thin Card

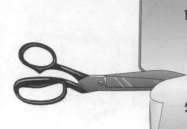

1) You can cut <u>paper</u> and <u>thin card</u> well with scissors — but they're not much good for <u>fine detail</u> or for <u>removing</u> bits from within a sheet of paper or card *(scalpels and knives are good for this — see below)*.

2) You can use '<u>pinking shears</u>' to produce an interesting <u>zigzag</u> edge (which also helps stop material from fraying).

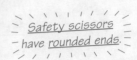
Safety scissors have <u>rounded ends</u>.

Craft Knives and Compass Cutters Cut Card and Paper

1) There are loads of different <u>craft</u>/<u>trimming</u>/<u>hobby knives</u>.

2) You mainly use these to cut <u>card</u> and <u>paper</u> — though some will cut thicker board, balsa wood, etc.

Surgical scalpels

These are <u>very sharp</u> and great for <u>precision</u> cutting.

Metal cased knife

<u>Stanley® knives</u>, and other 'generic' types. These are good for <u>tougher materials</u>, e.g. thick board or balsa wood.

Compass cutters

You use these to cut <u>arcs</u> and <u>circles</u> in card and paper. You can <u>vary</u> the <u>diameter</u> of the arc or circle to be cut.

Plastic trimming knife

Similar to the metal cased knife, but some have <u>retractable blades</u> or <u>blade covers</u> for <u>safety</u> when not in use. Many have <u>snap-off</u> blades, so you don't need to sharpen them.

Rotary Cutters and Guillotines Cut Large Sheets

1) You use <u>rotary cutters</u> (also known as rotatrims or paper trimmers) to cut large sheets of paper and card, often <u>many sheets at a time</u>.

2) They cut in a <u>straight line</u> to produce a nice straight edge.

<u>Guillotines</u> do the same thing, but they have a <u>large blade</u> that you push down.

My Stanley just wasn't sharp any more — so he got the chop...

<u>Take care</u> when cutting — not only will you get a better cut, you won't get <u>blood</u> on your work. Don't forget to use <u>cutting mats</u> and <u>metal rulers</u> with knives — they cut through tables and fingers too.

Tools

Modelling Materials Need Special Cutters

You might use <u>STYROFOAM</u>™, thin <u>plywood</u> or <u>MDF</u> in your models.

1) <u>STYROFOAM</u>™ is best cut with a <u>hot-wire cutter</u>.

2) A <u>fret saw</u> is useful for detailed cutting of <u>MDF</u> and <u>plywood</u> — it's really good when you need to cut <u>tight curves</u>.

3) <u>Plywood</u> and <u>MDF</u> are easily cut using a <u>coping saw</u>.

You Might Need to Fold or Bend After Cutting

1) <u>Die cutters</u> are commercial cutters a bit like pastry cutters. They're used to <u>cut out</u> materials for packaging (see page 49). You use <u>creasing bars</u> to add <u>creases</u> (no, really...), which make the material easier to fold.

2) If you need to bend <u>thermoplastics</u>, you can use a <u>line bender</u>.

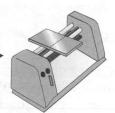

Safety Equipment is Really Important

When using cutting equipment, always take the right <u>safety precautions</u>.

1) When you're using a <u>craft knife</u> or any sharp cutting tool, it's best to use a <u>cutting mat</u> (to protect your work surface) and a <u>safety rule</u> (to protect your fingers).

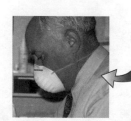

2) When cutting <u>STYROFOAM</u>™ or <u>MDF</u>, make sure there's plenty of <u>ventilation</u> and extraction — and wear a <u>mask</u> so that you don't breathe in the <u>dust</u>.

Mr Todd and Mr Blunt showed the class the safety precautions to take when working with MDF.

Practice Questions

1) What tool would you use to:
   a) remove a small shape from a piece of <u>card</u>?
   b) cut a <u>circle</u> from a piece of card?
   c) cut a piece of <u>balsa wood</u>?
   d) cut a <u>magazine</u> in half?

2) a) What would you use a <u>hot-wire cutter</u> for?
   b) Give an example of a product that might be made using a <u>die cutter</u>.

3) Name two pieces of <u>safety equipment</u> you should use when cutting straight lines in a piece of <u>balsa wood</u> using a knife.

4) What <u>safety precautions</u> should you take when cutting <u>MDF</u>?

Fixings and Bindings

Ooh, I do like a good <u>fixing</u>. Even if you don't share my enthusiasm, you still have to know about them.

Fixings Can Be Permanent...

1) <u>Double-sided sticky pads</u> will stick things together <u>quickly</u>.

2) <u>Ratchet rivets</u> and <u>rapid-assembly post and screw</u> fixings will join sheets of corrugated plastic together.

3) <u>Snap rivets</u> are plastic clips used to <u>join sheet material</u> (e.g. plastic) together. They're installed from <u>one side</u> — first you make a <u>hole</u> through the sheets then push the top of the rivet by hand.

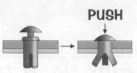

PUSH

...Or Temporary

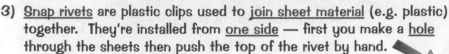

<u>Velcro®</u> <u>pads</u> are self-adhesive pieces of the <u>famous two-part</u> <u>hook and loop system</u>. They've got loads of uses — they're particularly good for displays.

Under a microscope the simplicity of Velcro® is easy to see.

<u>Press stud</u> <u>fastenings</u> are good for joining fabric bits together.

<u>Hooks</u> can be used to <u>hang</u> materials — they're useful when creating displays.

<u>Prong paper fasteners</u> join pieces of <u>paper</u> and <u>card</u> together as <u>movable joints</u>.

The fastener is inserted through a hole and then opened out.

<u>Treasury tags</u> hold stuff together <u>loosely</u>. They're really cheap.

<u>Drawing pins</u> (also known as <u>thumb tacks</u> or <u>mapping</u> <u>pins</u>) are useful for sticking paper and card to <u>display boards</u>.

<u>Staples</u> are a <u>permanent</u> or <u>temporary fixing</u> for paper or thin card. You can <u>remove</u> them with a <u>staple-remover</u>.

They know what staples are, Barney...

I can tell you're riveted by this page...

Yes, yes, I know — you know most of this already. But, really, don't overlook the humble staple — think about all of the times it's saved your life. Probably just as many times as the little old paper clip.

Fixings and Bindings

Bindings hold <u>sheets of paper</u> together. There are lots of different types — which one you choose depends on <u>cost</u>, the <u>number</u> of sheets you need to hold and the <u>appearance</u> you want.

Some Bindings are Cheap and Cheerful...

1) In `comb binding` you <u>punch holes</u> in the sheets using a special <u>machine</u>, then put a <u>plastic comb</u> in. You can <u>add or remove</u> pages without causing damage and the bound book <u>opens flat</u>, making it <u>easy to read</u>.

2) In `spiral binding` a <u>plastic coil</u> is inserted down the spine. <u>Wiro binding</u> is similar to spiral but it uses a <u>double loop wire</u> instead of a plastic coil.

comb binding   spiral binding   wiro binding

3) `Saddle stitching` is where double sized pages are <u>folded</u> and <u>stapled</u> together at the centre. This type of binding is easy and cheap but it <u>won't hold many sheets</u>. Saddle stitched books open more or less <u>flat</u>. <u>This very book</u> you're reading now is saddle stitched.

...and Some are a Bit More Expensive

1) In `perfect binding`, pages are folded together in <u>sections</u>. Each section is <u>roughened</u> at the fold and then <u>glued</u> to the <u>spine</u>. You can bind <u>lots of sheets</u> but you can't open the book <u>flat</u>.

2) `Thread-sewing` is <u>expensive</u>. The pages are <u>sewn</u> together in sections, then a <u>soft cover</u> is <u>glued</u> on. The pages are less likely to come <u>loose</u> than with perfect binding.

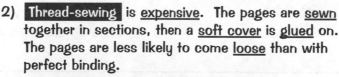

3) `Case-Bound/Hard-Bound` books are like <u>thread-sewn</u> ones but with a <u>hard cover</u>.

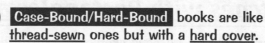

<u>Index tabs</u> help to sort a book into sections, making it <u>easier to find</u> parts because <u>flaps stick out</u>.

Practice Questions

1) Name three types of <u>permanent fixing</u>.

2) Tim is designing a <u>booklet</u> in which the pages will be fixed together at one corner. He then wants to attach the booklet to a <u>display board</u>.
   a) Name <u>two</u> types of <u>temporary fixing</u> that Tim could use to loosely hold together the sheets of paper in his booklet.
   b) How could Tim attach his booklet to a <u>display board</u>?

3) Dave needs to bind some copies of his design evaluation. He needs ten copies for his classmates and one copy for his teacher.
   a) Suggest how Dave could <u>cheaply</u> and <u>quickly</u> bind ten copies for his classmates.
   b) He binds his teacher's copy using <u>thread-sewing</u>. Give one <u>advantage</u> of thread sewing over perfect binding.

Sketching

You <u>don't always</u> have to use <u>perfect</u> drawings. <u>Freehand sketches</u> are fine for getting across <u>initial ideas</u>. And they're pretty <u>easy</u> to do — so you can get <u>new thoughts</u> on paper <u>quickly</u>.

Freehand Sketching is Very Quick

1) <u>Freehand drawing</u> is where you <u>don't</u> use any <u>drawing equipment</u> apart from a pencil or pen.

2) It's the <u>quickest</u> method of drawing and is handy for getting <u>initial ideas</u> down on paper.

EXAM TIP
Use freehand sketches when you're coming up with initial design ideas.

Ideas for a space themed birthday card.

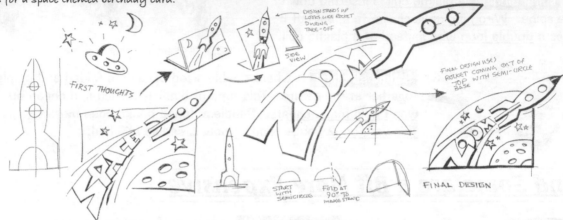

3) You can <u>combine 2D</u> and <u>3D</u> sketches to show details.

4) And you can add <u>notes</u> to explain details, e.g. ideas for colours and materials.

5) <u>3D</u> freehand sketches often show how the <u>whole object</u> would look, while <u>2D</u> drawings tend to show the <u>details</u> of an object.

Start 2D Sketches with Rectangles and Squares

Standard <u>sketching</u> is very similar to <u>freehand</u> sketching, except that you start by <u>ruling guidelines</u>.

1) Using <u>vertical</u> and <u>horizontal</u> lines you can create squares and rectangles.

2) Use these to draw the <u>outline</u> of your shape first.

3) Details can be added by drawing more <u>squares</u> and <u>rectangles</u>.

4) Add <u>circles</u> and <u>ellipses</u> where necessary.

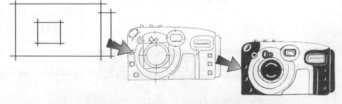

- Use <u>square boxes</u> to draw <u>circles</u> and <u>rectangular boxes</u> to draw <u>ellipses</u>.
- Mark <u>half way</u> along each side.
- <u>Join the points</u> to form the circle or ellipse.

EXAM TIP
Use guidelines when you need to sketch accurately — e.g. when drawing the final version of a logo.

If you've got a freehand, could you just help me with this...

And you thought sketching was just for doodling in the margins of your work... Make sure you get the hang of <u>crating</u> (see the next page). But don't do it for every sketch — freehand is much <u>quicker</u>.

Sketching

Draw More Accurately Using a Grid

1) You can lay <u>grids</u> under your page to improve the <u>accuracy</u> of your drawing.
   (Or you could just draw on graph/grid paper.)

2) You could use an <u>isometric</u> grid, <u>perspective</u> grid or a <u>square</u> grid.

 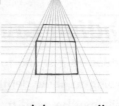 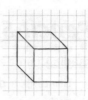

      isometric   one-point perspective   square grid

Crating Can Be Used to Draw 3D Shapes

<u>Crating</u> is where you start by drawing a box — the 'crate' — and gradually <u>add bits</u> on and <u>take bits off</u> till you get the right shape. For example, you can <u>remove sections</u> from a cuboid to make <u>any</u> other 3D shape.

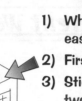

1) When you're sketching a 3D object, it's easier if you imagine it as a <u>basic shape</u>.

2) First draw the <u>basic geometric shape</u> faintly.

3) Stick to a particular drawing technique like <u>two-point perspective</u> or <u>isometric</u> (p.42-43).

4) The object can then be drawn <u>within the box</u>.

5) <u>Details</u> of the object can be added by drawing more <u>geometric shapes</u> on top.

Crating Produces Wireframe Drawings

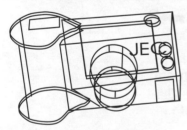

1) When you draw using the crating technique you can leave the solid sides of the shape <u>unshaded</u>.

2) Doing this lets you see <u>straight through</u> the object, as with this camera.

3) Wireframe can be used to show details on <u>all faces</u> of an object.

4) You can also view objects in <u>wireframe</u> in <u>CAD software</u>.

Practice Questions

1) a) What is <u>freehand drawing</u>?
   b) Suggest what you'd use it for.
   c) Why is it a good idea to <u>annotate</u> freehand sketches?

2) Draw an <u>ellipse</u> 40 mm wide and 70 mm long using guidelines.

3) a) Draw a cuboid with dimensions 30 mm × 30 mm × 40 mm using <u>isometric paper</u>.
   b) Suggest another type of grid that could be used for drawing in 3D.

4) a) What is <u>crating</u>?
   b) Draw a design for a <u>radio</u> using crating.
   c) What type of drawing does crating produce if the solid sides of the shape are left <u>unshaded</u>?

Shading and Texture

You can use various techniques to <u>enhance</u> a final presentation drawing. You can change the <u>thickness of lines</u> or add <u>shading</u> to make parts of the drawing <u>stand out</u>. Then there's always <u>colour</u>...

Pencil Shading Can be Used to Accentuate Shape

<u>Shading</u> can be added to a shape to make it look <u>3D</u>.

1) Shading a drawing to show <u>depth</u>, <u>light and shade</u> or <u>texture</u> is called <u>rendering</u>.

2) Different <u>pencils</u> can be used to create different <u>tones</u> — darker or lighter.

3) A <u>soft pencil</u> can create a wide <u>range of tones</u>.

4) Think about where the light's coming from — make areas <u>furthest</u> from the light the <u>darkest</u>.

LIGHT

LIGHT

You Can Use a Pencil to Shade in Different Ways

There are several different shading techniques. Here are four common ones:

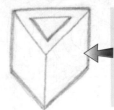

If you can see <u>both surfaces</u> that form a line, draw it <u>thin</u>. If you can only see <u>one surface</u>, draw a <u>thick line</u>. This gives the impression of solidity.

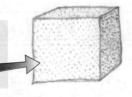

Use <u>highlights</u> to suggest a <u>reflective</u> surface. Add them by leaving <u>white</u> areas.

You can shade using <u>dots</u> — just use a <u>different concentration of dots</u> on each side. It's pretty <u>time-consuming</u> though.

You can also shade using <u>lines</u>. You need to use <u>lines at different spacing</u> on each side. Lines at <u>different angles</u> can be used to show different colours, materials, etc.

For Wood Use Colour and Draw a Grain

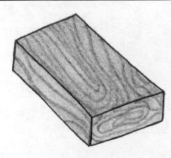

1) <u>Wood</u> can be drawn using <u>coloured pencils</u> to represent the <u>colour</u> and <u>grain</u>.

2) You can use more than one colour to get the <u>right shade</u>.

3) <u>Wood grain</u> can be added using a <u>darker</u> pencil. Remember that the <u>side</u> grain and the <u>end</u> grain look <u>different</u>.

Don't forget to draw the grain.

Keep out of the sun — do some shading...

These techniques usually take a bit of <u>practice</u> — but this is Graphic Products, so they're pretty useful. They'll make your sketches look more <u>realistic</u>, which is useful for getting your design ideas across.

Shading and Texture

Draw the Reflections if Metal is Shiny

1) <u>Metals</u> can have a variety of colours and finishes.
2) You could have flat <u>sheet metal</u>, or metal with a <u>texture</u>.
3) <u>Textured metal</u> can be represented using <u>line techniques</u>, e.g. drawing lines to show any ridges, bumps etc.
4) When shading <u>shiny metal</u> look closely at what the <u>reflections</u> actually look like — and use <u>highlights</u> to show them.

There Are a Few Tricks for Plastic

1) <u>Marker pens</u> are useful for creating the look of <u>plastic</u>. Alternatively you could use soft <u>coloured pencils</u> or <u>poster paints</u>.

2) <u>Pale</u> coloured <u>marker pens</u>, <u>watercolour paints or pencils</u> or <u>coloured pencils</u> can be used to make an object appear <u>transparent</u>. You may even see other objects through the transparent object.

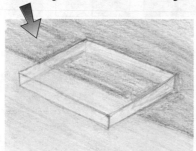

3) Most <u>dark</u> colours look opaque (not see-through) automatically, but you could make a <u>pale</u> coloured material look <u>opaque</u> using <u>watercolour paints</u> by adding a bit of yellow.

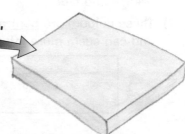

Practice Questions

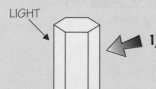

LIGHT

1) Copy the shape on the left. Use a <u>pencil</u> to shade it to make it look 3D.

2) Copy the cube on the right. Use <u>thick and thin lines</u> to make it look solid.

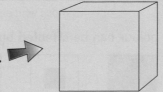

3) Suggest what techniques and equipment you'd use to draw a <u>block of wood</u>.

4) What technique could you use to show the <u>reflections</u> in metal?

5) a) Suggest two pieces of drawing equipment you could use to create the look of <u>plastic</u>.
   b) Suggest a way of making a pale coloured material look <u>opaque</u>.

Colour and Mood

Understanding the <u>colour wheel</u> is important when you're producing design sketches and drawings. Learn what colours <u>go together</u> and what combinations to <u>avoid</u> — just make sure it doesn't run you over.

Colours Can be Organised into Different Groups

There are two main groups of colours — <u>primary</u> and <u>secondary</u>.

1) The <u>primary colours</u> — red , blue and yellow — can be mixed together to produce many other colours.

2) <u>Secondary colours</u> — orange , purple and green — are colours made by <u>mixing</u> together primary colours. For example, <u>orange</u> is made by mixing together <u>yellow</u> and <u>red</u>.

3) Colour can be represented on a <u>colour wheel</u> which shows you how all the colours <u>fit together</u>. The <u>secondary colours</u> are made by mixing the primary colours on <u>either side</u> of them.

orange = red + yellow

purple = red + blue

green = yellow + blue

This colour wheel only applies to <u>paint</u> or <u>pigments</u> — not to <u>light</u>.
(The primary colours for light are red, green and blue, which gives a different set of secondary colours too.)

Complementary Colours Are Contrasting

1) <u>Complementary</u> colours are found <u>opposite</u> each other on the <u>colour wheel</u> — green and red, purple and yellow and orange and blue.

2) These colours are <u>contrasting</u> — they stand out against each other and can seem more <u>intense</u> than when they're on their own.

In <u>CAD packages</u> you can <u>select</u> and <u>change</u> colours really easily. But if you're drawing by <u>hand</u> and you want to change the colours, you'll have to start your drawing again.

EXAM TIP
Think about which colours go together well — you don't want to have to start your drawing again.

Colours Have Different Hues and Tones

1) <u>Hue</u> is just another word for <u>colour</u> — it's the <u>actual</u> colour (e.g. red, green, orange, etc.).

2) The <u>tone</u> of a colour (how <u>dark or light</u> it is) can be changed by adding <u>black or white</u> to it. For example, blue can have different tones, e.g. light blue, royal blue or navy blue.

more white

3) The way you <u>perceive</u> a colour can be affected by its <u>surroundings</u>.

4) The red stands out <u>vibrantly</u> against the black and green backgrounds. However, the red looks a bit <u>duller</u> against the orange and white.

It's best to avoid using red and green together — the most common type of colour-blindness is red/green.

Car for sale — five gears, 0-60 in 5.6 seconds, colour wheels...

You need to pick the colours of your product wisely — you can't just spin the colour wheel and pick out <u>any old colour</u>. As you're about to find out on the next page, colours can have different meanings.

Colour and Mood

Colours Can be Used to Represent Mood

Colour is often used in graphic products to represent different <u>moods</u> or <u>feelings</u>.

To create a <u>heavy</u> mood, you might use a <u>dark solid colour</u>...

...while for a <u>lighter</u> mood you'd go for a <u>paler colour</u>.

Colours such as <u>red</u> and <u>orange</u> remind us of <u>fire</u> and the <u>sun</u> and so are known as <u>warm colours</u>...

...whereas <u>blues</u> are normally associated with <u>cold</u>.

Colours such as <u>blue</u> and <u>purple</u> remind us of <u>water</u> and the <u>sky</u> and are known as <u>cool colours</u> — these are generally quite calming colours.

With all this green I feel so serene.

Colours you find in <u>nature</u> such as <u>browns</u>, <u>greys</u> and <u>greens</u> are known as <u>neutral colours</u>. They're also associated with <u>calm</u> or <u>relaxation</u>.

On the other hand, <u>red</u> often represents <u>anger</u> and <u>conflict</u> and can symbolise <u>danger</u>.

Practice Questions

1) a) What are the two main <u>groups</u> of colours?
   b) Name the three colours in each group

2) Look at the colour wheel on the left.
   a) Which two colours should be mixed together to make <u>purple</u>?
   b) Which two colours should be mixed together to make <u>green</u>?

3) a) What is meant by the '<u>tone</u>' of a colour?
   b) How is the tone of a colour <u>changed</u>?

4) a) How would you use colour to suggest a <u>lighter mood</u> in a product?
   b) List two <u>calming</u> colours.
   c) Why are road signs giving <u>warnings</u> coloured <u>red</u>?

Colour Fusion and Separation

Before we dive into colour fusion and separation, there are a few bits and pieces you should know first...

Colour Printers Use Four Colours in Layers

1) Colour printers use four colours — cyan, magenta, yellow and black (CMYK).
   The 'K' stands for 'key' — it means black. You can make black by mixing the other three colours, but using black ink usually looks better, and it works out cheaper if you're printing a lot of black.

2) Anything that's printed in colour is made up of a mixture of these colours.

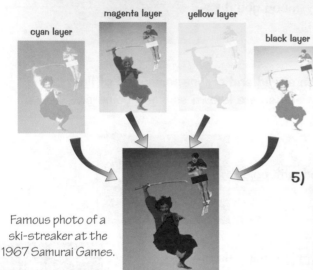

cyan layer
magenta layer
yellow layer
black layer

Famous photo of a ski-streaker at the 1967 Samurai Games.

3) When the computer is instructed to print, the printer recognises the required colour and adds layers of cyan, magenta, yellow and black to make the final colour.

4) Some printers use special spot colours (e.g. PANTONE® colours) as well — to print particular colours that can't be achieved with CMYK.

5) Spot colours might be used to make images look more realistic, e.g. for metallic colours and flesh tones in photos of people. Some companies that use particular colours as part of their branding also use spot colours, because they always come out exactly the same whatever printer you use.

Screen Printing Also Uses Layers of Colour

1) When screen printing you also add colour in layers.
2) These layers build up to produce the final colour.
3) This is the traditional system of colouring paper and cloth.

The screen is made of a very fine mesh held taut around a strong wooden frame.

To print a design, you lop a load of dye cream onto the mesh, then pull across a rubber squeegee to push the dye through the mesh.

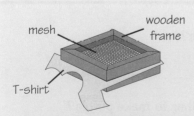

mesh
wooden frame

T-shirt

CGP

A stencil is put underneath the mesh. The material you're going to print onto is put under the stencil.

The dye will only go through the gaps in the stencil...

...so you get a pretty pattern on your T-shirt.

Black begins with a B — can't they spell...

Colour printing is a pretty clever thing. And it makes sense to mix four layers of colour, really — think how big printers would need to be if they had to contain cartridges of every single colour.

Colour Fusion and Separation

Screen printing is fine, but there are more <u>modern</u> ways of printing your design.

Colour Fusion is all About Blending

1) <u>Colour fusion</u> happens when tiny dots of different colours really close together appear to blend into a new, single colour. For example, <u>yellow</u> and <u>blue</u> dots close together will look <u>green</u>.

2) This printing technique is used a lot in <u>advertising posters</u>, <u>leaflets</u> and <u>newspapers</u>. Newspapers are usually printed at <u>150 dpi</u> (dots per inch). You can see the dots if you look <u>really, really close</u>.

3) It's also how <u>television screens</u> work.

one pixel

- Pictures on a TV screen are made from the colours <u>red</u>, <u>green</u> and <u>blue</u> (RGB for short, though you'd never have guessed).
- The screen is made up of thousands of tiny coloured <u>pixels</u> (dots).
- Each tiny pixel consists of a red, green and blue <u>bar</u>. The <u>intensity</u> of each of these bars produces the <u>final pixel colour</u> you see. Dead clever.

Colour Separation, Well, Separates the Colours

If you've <u>hand-drawn</u> your design, you can print a full colour image of it.
You just need to use a <u>digital scanner</u>. This <u>separates</u> your drawing into different colours — red, green and blue:

1) The scanner uses <u>colour filters</u> which only let one colour through — either red, green or blue.

2) It takes <u>three pictures</u> of the image at the same time, each using a different colour filter.

3) Graphics software (or sometimes the printer itself) <u>converts</u> the RGB scan to <u>CMYK data</u> for printing. Instructions are sent to the <u>printer</u> about the CMYK colours needed for the image. The printer then prints the image by adding these four colours in layers.

4) If you've drawn your design using <u>CAD</u>, the printer can separate the colours — it has <u>colour separation software</u> built in.

Practice Questions

1) a) List the <u>four colours</u> that colour printers use.
   b) Outline how colour printers create <u>other colours</u>.
   c) Colour printers sometimes use 'spot colours'. What are these used for?

2) Vijay wants to print a design onto a tea towel using screen printing.
   a) Outline how he would <u>set up</u> the apparatus.
   b) Outline how he would <u>print</u> the design onto the towel.

3) a) What is <u>colour fusion</u>?
   b) Name two things that this printing technique is used for.

4) Steve has just bought a new TV. The manual outlines how the <u>screen works</u>. Suggest what it might say.

5) Philippa has hand-drawn her design. She uses a <u>digital scanner</u> so that she can print out a full-colour image. What does the digital scanner do?

Lettering and Presentation

Computers make it really easy to manipulate images — you can fiddle about editing stuff till the cows come home. It's all about making your design look professional for when you present it to other people.

You Need to Present Your Final Design

When designers are completely satisfied with a design, they'll have to present it to the client.
You'll have to do presentation drawings in the exam and for your project too.

1) Good presentation drawings are really important — it helps the client (or in your case, the examiner) to clearly visualise the product.

2) You should ideally have two different types of presentation drawing:

 • A 3D drawing showing how the finished product will look.

 • A working drawing with dimensions and other details, e.g. materials and finishes.
   The client will probably want to see this one too — and the manufacturer definitely needs it.

3) Presentation drawings can be done using CAD — you can make them look very realistic by adding texture and light effects.

4) Neat, hand-drawn presentation drawings are also fine. The downside of doing this in industry is that the designer would have to re-draw it if the client wanted them to make any alterations.

Once the client has given the design the thumbs up, you need to think about advertising the product to potential customers. You can create advertisements using ICT and CAD — and there are plenty of effects you can use to make the product look appealing (see below).

EXAM TIP
You'll have to do a final presentation drawing in your exam — make sure it's really neat and uses colour and shading.

Images Can Be Manipulated

Using CAD packages (see page 62) you can produce and edit drawings of a product.
It's easy to show the client the designs and they can specify any changes before manufacturing.
The images can be manipulated in a number of ways.

1) You can alter colours easily and add special light and shadow effects, e.g. to make metal look like it's gleaming.

2) You can show details of dimensions and materials.

3) Doing simple things like changing the background can make a big difference — make the most of using computer effects to make your presentation drawing stand out.

Other computer software can be used to manipulate photographs,
e.g. Paint Shop Pro and Adobe® Photoshop®.

1) Colours can be altered easily, and special effects can be added. For example, photos can be edited so that they look distorted or to make them look like pencil drawings.

2) These techniques are widely used in products such as posters and leaflets, and on websites.

You need to add lettering to your exam paper too...

...but that won't be a problem once you've learnt this. One word of advice though — I wouldn't do your exam by using CAD and getting it cut out with a laser cutter. I'd stick to the old pen and paper.

Lettering and Presentation

Lettering Can Be Added to Products

1) Lettering varies from <u>ornate</u>, <u>traditional styles</u> to <u>modern</u>, <u>dynamic</u> styles.

2) Different lettering styles (fonts) are used for different <u>purposes</u>.

3) A <u>traditional</u> font, e.g. one with <u>serifs</u> or a <u>script</u> style wouldn't really be suitable for a <u>trendy</u>, <u>up-to-date</u> product.

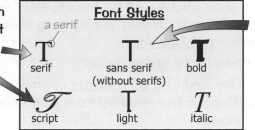

Font Styles

a serif

T — serif

T — sans serif (without serifs)

T — bold

T — script

T — light

T — italic

4) In the same way, very <u>modern</u> fonts (these are mostly <u>sans serif</u> fonts) would look out of place on a product with a <u>traditional</u>, <u>old-fashioned look</u>.

5) Lettering can be created <u>by hand</u> or using <u>CAD</u>.

6) Lettering designed using a <u>CAD package</u> can be sent to a <u>CAM machine</u>, e.g. <u>a laser cutter</u>, to be produced. This allows you to cut <u>very accurate</u> lettering from, say, sheets of acrylic.

Paper Can be Protected by Encapsulation

It's important to <u>protect</u> your finished product. If it's a paper product, it can be protected by <u>encapsulating</u> (enclosing) it in a <u>sealed pocket</u>. This will also make it <u>look better</u> — you could encapsulate any drawings that you want to show to the client.

1) Encapsulation is done using a <u>laminating machine</u>.

2) The paper product is <u>laid between</u> two sheets of clear plastic.

3) This sandwich is then inserted into the laminating machine. The machine <u>heats</u> the plastic and <u>seals</u> in the paper.

4) Things like <u>brochures</u> and <u>menus</u> can be laminated on one or both sides using gloss or matt laminate.

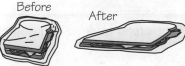

Before

After

Don't try this with a real sandwich...

Practice Questions

1) a) What are <u>presentation drawings</u> used for?
   b) Give two types of presentation drawing.

2) What is the disadvantage of doing presentation drawings <u>by hand</u>?

3) Suggest two ways that <u>CAD</u> packages can be used to manipulate design images.

4) Suggest two ways that <u>photographs</u> can be manipulated using computer software.

5) Say whether the font is serif or sans serif: a) Trout   b) Chump   c) Turnips

6) Jenny is designing a brochure for tourists visiting the ruins of an abbey. What <u>type of font</u> might she use? Explain your answer.

7) What type of <u>CAM machine</u> could be used to <u>produce lettering</u> for a plastic product?

8) Tony has printed some <u>paper menus</u> for his restaurant.
   a) What technique could he use to <u>protect</u> the menus?
   b) Outline how this would be done.

Pictorial Drawings

Pictorial drawing is just a fancy way of saying 'drawing in 3D'. You can really show off your design ideas with these techniques — flippin' useful stuff if you ask me.

Perspective Drawing Uses Vanishing Points

1) Perspective drawing tries to show what something actually looks like — smaller in the distance, larger close to. It does this by using lines that appear to meet at points called vanishing points.

2) These points are in the distance on the horizon line.

3) Perspective drawing is great for producing 3D drawings of products, packaging and point-of-sale displays (eye-catching sales promotions you find near check-out counters).

Use One-Point Perspective to Draw Objects Head On

1) One-point perspective only uses one vanishing point.

2) For example, here's how to draw a cube using one-point perspective.

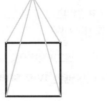

1) Mark one vanishing point.

2) Draw the front view of the object head on.

3) Then draw lines connecting the corners to the vanishing point.

4) Use these lines to complete the 3D shape. Hey presto.

3) You could use the same four steps to draw any object in one-point perspective.

Use Two-Point Perspective to Draw Objects at an Angle

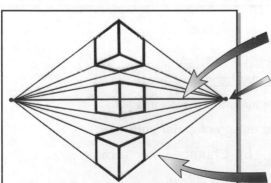

Two-point perspective shows objects edge-on.

1) Draw a horizon line horizontally across the page.

2) Mark two vanishing points — one at each end of the horizon line.

3) Draw the object by starting with the front, vertical edge and then projecting lines to the vanishing points.

4) Remember that vertical lines remain vertical and all horizontal lines go to one of the vanishing points.

5) The object appears different depending on whether it's drawn above, below or on the horizon line.

Don't worry about your drawings — get some perspective...

These techniques can be used to draw all sorts of things, but the only way to get good at using them is to practise. To make your drawings even more realistic, try out the shading techniques in section 3.

Pictorial Drawings

Isometric Drawing Shows Objects at 30°

1) Isometric drawing can be used to show an object in <u>3D</u>.

2) It <u>doesn't show perspective</u> (things don't get smaller in the distance), but it's <u>easier to get dimensions</u> right than in perspective drawing.

3) Isometric drawing shows <u>three sides</u> of the object. It's useful for drawing <u>products</u> and their <u>packaging</u>.

4) There are <u>three main rules</u> when doing isometric drawings:

> •   Vertical edges are drawn as vertical lines.
> •   Horizontal edges are drawn at 30°.
> •   Parallel edges appear as parallel lines.

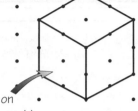

This drawing's been done on isometric <u>grid paper</u>. You could use plain paper and a <u>30°/60°</u> <u>set square</u> instead.

You can also draw more <u>complicated</u> shapes, e.g. <u>circles</u>:

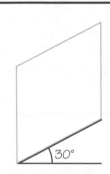

1) Start off by drawing an <u>isometric crate</u> — a 'square' skewed by 30°. (Draw it faintly — it's only a guide.)

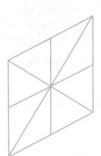

2) Divide the crate up <u>horizontally</u>, <u>vertically</u> and <u>diagonally</u>.

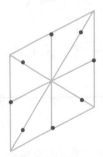

3) Use these lines to help you <u>mark out</u> a circle with dots.

4) <u>Join</u> up the dots to <u>draw</u> your circle.

Practice Questions

1) Name two <u>3D</u> drawing techniques.

2) What is a <u>vanishing point</u>?

3) A company wants you to design a point-of-sale display for their new chocolate bar.
   a) Sketch the outline of a chocolate bar using <u>one-point perspective</u>.
   b) Now draw it <u>above</u> the horizon line using <u>two-point perspective</u>.

4) Bob is doing an isometric drawing.
   At what <u>angle</u> should he draw the horizontal edges of the object?

5) Fred wants to advertise his new board game with a picture of a dice.
   a) What kind of drawing should he use to show <u>three sides</u> of the dice with the <u>right dimensions</u>?
   b) Draw a <u>dice</u> using the technique named in part a).

Working Drawings

Once you've <u>perfected</u> your <u>design idea</u>, you'll need to produce an <u>accurate working drawing</u> so that the manufacturer can make it. So guess what's coming up on these pages...

Orthographic Projection Shows 2D Views of a 3D Object

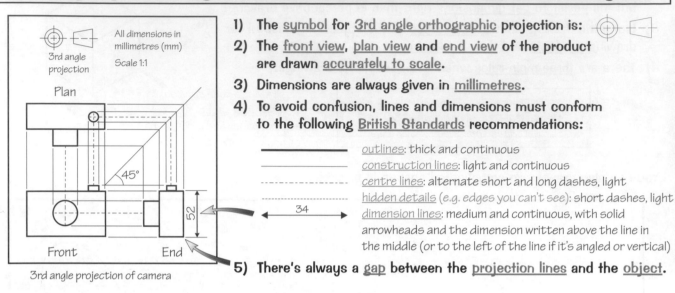

3rd angle projection
All dimensions in millimetres (mm)
Scale 1:1

Plan

45°

52

34

Front   End

3rd angle projection of camera

1) The <u>symbol</u> for <u>3rd angle orthographic</u> projection is:

2) The <u>front view</u>, <u>plan view</u> and <u>end view</u> of the product are drawn <u>accurately to scale</u>.

3) Dimensions are always given in <u>millimetres</u>.

4) To avoid confusion, lines and dimensions must conform to the following <u>British Standards</u> recommendations:

   <u>outlines</u>: thick and continuous
   <u>construction lines</u>: light and continuous
   <u>centre lines</u>: alternate short and long dashes, light
   <u>hidden details</u> (e.g. edges you can't see): short dashes, light
   <u>dimension lines</u>: medium and continuous, with solid arrowheads and the dimension written above the line in the middle (or to the left of the line if it's angled or vertical)

5) There's always a <u>gap</u> between the <u>projection lines</u> and the <u>object</u>.

To draw a 3rd angle orthographic projection, you:

1) Draw the <u>front view</u>.
2) Add construction lines going <u>up</u> to draw the <u>plan view</u>.
3) Add construction lines to the <u>right</u> to draw the <u>end view</u>.
4) Add the <u>dimensions</u> — don't forget to use <u>millimetres</u>.
5) Feel dead chuffed at how <u>professional</u> it looks.

3rd angle projections are used very widely in industry to help the manufacturer understand the design.

Exploded Views Show Separate Parts

There are a few ways of showing how things <u>fit together</u> — one is to show an <u>exploded view</u>.

1) Exploded views are always in <u>3D</u>.
2) You draw the product with <u>each separate part</u> of it <u>moved out</u> as if it's been exploded.
3) Each part of the product is <u>drawn in line</u> with the part it's attached to.
4) Dotted lines show where the part has been <u>exploded from</u>.

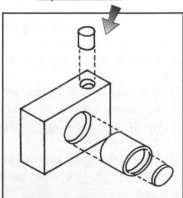

Exploded view of a camera

As well as being sent to the manufacturer, exploded drawings are often used for <u>flat-pack furniture instructions</u> — see the next page.

Blowing stuff up doesn't make exploded views easier...

...and you'll probably get into some serious trouble. Anyway, the <u>3rd angle</u> stuff will come in useful for your <u>project</u>. You need to put in <u>enough info</u> so that a manufacturer could make your product.

Working Drawings

Self-Assembly Drawings are Often Exploded Views

1) The <u>self-assembly drawings</u> you find with flat pack furniture are often <u>exploded views</u>.
   This is because they show <u>clearly</u> how the different parts should fit together.

2) Self-assembly drawings should be <u>labelled</u> — but good ones <u>don't need</u> too many <u>words</u>.
   The whole idea is that the pictures should be <u>easy to follow</u> on their own (and then the same instructions can be used in <u>any country</u> because <u>language</u> doesn't matter).

3) Instructions often use a whole <u>series</u> of exploded views — they should be <u>numbered</u> to show the order.

Sectional Drawings Show Internal Details

1) Sectional drawings show what the product would look like inside if you <u>cut it in two</u>.

2) A <u>front view</u> of the object shows <u>where</u> the 'cut' has been made.
   In this diagram of a camera it's been cut through section XY.

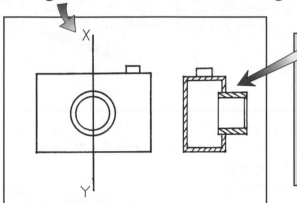

- <u>Cross-hatched lines</u> are used to show where the product has been 'cut'.
- The hatching is normally drawn at a <u>45° angle</u> with the lines <u>evenly</u> spaced.
- <u>Different parts</u> are hatched in a <u>different way</u>. In this diagram the lines are running in <u>opposite directions</u>.

Sectional drawing of a camera

3) Sometimes more than one section is shown, so each section line must be <u>labelled</u> very clearly.

Practice Questions

1) When you're adding dimensions to a drawing, what <u>units</u> should they be in?

2) What are the <u>three views</u> you need to draw when doing a 3rd angle orthographic projection of an object?

3) a) Suggest a type of drawing that is suitable for <u>self-assembly</u> instructions.
   b) Explain why this type of drawing is suitable.

4) a) What kind of drawing shows you the <u>internal details</u> of an object?
   b) Draw this washing machine as if you were looking at it <u>cut in two</u> through section X,Y.
   c) Add some <u>cross-hatching</u> to your drawing, to show where the washing machine has been 'cut'.

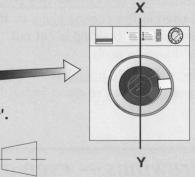

5) What does this <u>symbol</u> mean?
   A   1st Angle Scout Brigade
   B   3rd angle orthographic projection
   C   wash at 30 °C

Working Drawings

Working 9:5 — what a way to scale a drawing.

Scale Drawings are Used to Draw Big Things (but smaller)

1) To draw a <u>big object</u> on a small piece of paper, you have to <u>scale it down</u>.

2) The object's still drawn in <u>proportion</u> — it's just <u>smaller</u>.

3) The <u>scale</u> is shown as a <u>ratio</u>. For example:

> - A scale of <u>1:2</u> means that the <u>drawing</u> is <u>half the size</u> of the <u>real object</u>.
> - A scale of <u>1:4</u> means that the drawing is <u>a quarter of the size</u> of the real object.
> - Anything drawn at <u>1:1</u> is <u>full sized</u>.

4) The <u>scale</u> needs to be <u>clearly</u> shown on the diagram. It's a ratio, so it <u>doesn't have any units</u>.

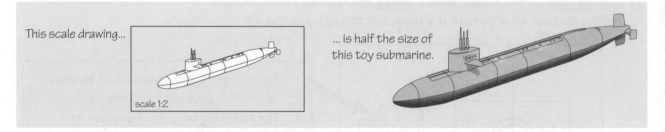

This scale drawing...

scale 1:2

... is half the size of this toy submarine.

5) To <u>check</u> you've scaled an object down properly, <u>measure</u> the lengths of the lines in your <u>drawing</u>. If you <u>multiply</u> those lengths <u>by the scale</u>, you should get the dimensions of the <u>real object</u>.

6) Lines on a scale drawing should be labelled with the <u>lengths</u> of the <u>real object</u> — <u>not</u> the lengths of the lines on the paper.

You can also scale things up. A scale of 2:1 means the drawing is twice the size of the real object.

Room and Site Plans are Drawn to Scale

1) A <u>room plan</u> is a <u>scale drawing</u> of a room <u>from above</u> — it shows all the features, like doors and windows.

This is the real length of the room — <u>not</u> the length of the room in the drawing.

4.5 m

3.5 m

Scale 1:100

2) A <u>floor plan</u> shows <u>one whole floor of a building</u>. They're often used in <u>fire escape plans</u> so that people can see how the building is set out. Again, they're drawn to scale.

3) <u>Site plans</u> (also called <u>site maps</u>) show a <u>construction site</u> from above. Builders can see <u>what</u> they're going to build and <u>where</u> they're going to build it.

Working drawings — even graphics have to earn a living...

Working drawings are all about <u>conveying information</u> — usually between the <u>designer</u> and the person <u>making</u> the product. That information has <u>got to be accurate</u> — or the product won't get made right.

Working Drawings

Schematic Drawings Aren't Drawn to Scale

1) <u>Schematic drawings</u> clearly show the layout of <u>electrical</u> and <u>mechanical</u> systems.

2) They have lots of uses — for example, to show a <u>manufacturer</u> how to <u>make an electrical device</u>, or to tell a <u>plumber</u> the <u>layout of piping</u> in a house.

3) The <u>circuit diagram</u> on the right is an example of a basic schematic diagram.

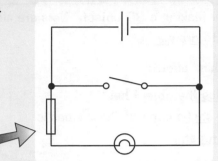

Schematic Maps Show Transport Systems

1) <u>Harry Beck's</u> map of the <u>London Underground</u> (see page 6) is an example of a <u>schematic map</u>.

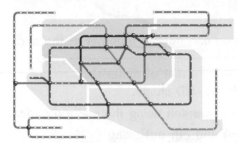

A schematic map of bus routes in a city.

2) His map is <u>non-geographical</u> — it just shows the <u>order</u> of the stations coming up <u>next</u>, and spaces them out evenly to make the map easier to read.

3) Lots of different <u>transport networks</u> (e.g. bus routes and the motorway system) use this idea in their maps because it's <u>clear</u> and <u>simple</u>.

4) Different motorways and bus routes can be shown in <u>different colours</u>.

Practice Questions

1) What are <u>scale drawings</u> used for?

2) a) What does this mean?

scale 1:4

? mm

b) What is this measurement in real life?

3) Sketch a <u>1:2</u> scale drawing of the pen or pencil you're using to answer these questions.

4) a) What is a <u>room plan</u>?
   b) Give one use of a <u>floor plan</u>.
   c) Why does the construction industry use <u>site plans</u>?

5) Betty catches bus number 66 into town. This is the geographical route taken by the bus.
   a) Draw a <u>schematic map</u> of the bus route.
   b) Suggest why Betty might find it <u>easier</u> to use the schematic map.

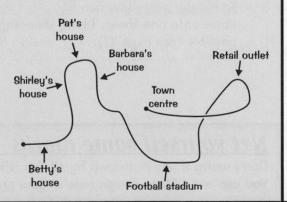

Nets and Packaging

Everything you ever wanted to know about <u>surfaces</u>. Apart from the surface of the moon.

3D Objects Can be Made from 2D Nets

A <u>net</u> is a <u>2D</u> plan for making a <u>3D</u> object. Nets are also called <u>surface developments</u>.
You need to be able to <u>draw a net</u>...

Just remember to think about:

- how many <u>sides</u> the object has
- what <u>size</u> and <u>shape</u> each of these sides is
- how it all <u>fits together</u>

It might help to <u>imagine unfolding</u> your object.

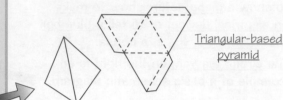

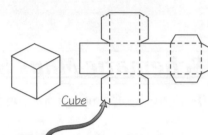

Triangular-based pyramid

When drawing a net, use:

- <u>solid lines</u> to show which edges you're supposed to <u>cut</u>
- <u>dotted</u> or <u>dashed lines</u> to show which edges to <u>fold</u>

Cube

Don't forget to include <u>tabs</u> in the design of your net — so that you can <u>stick it together</u> at the end.

1) Nets are great for <u>modelling ideas</u>. You <u>draw</u> the net onto a flat sheet of material (e.g. paper, card, acrylic) and then <u>cut</u> it out and <u>fold</u> it into the 3D shape.

2) A lot of <u>packaging</u> is made from nets — you can make some yourself using the method above.

3) In <u>industry</u>, the net would be designed with <u>CAD</u> (see below) and cut out using <u>CAM</u> (see next page). It'd then be <u>folded</u> and <u>stuck together</u>.

CAD Can be Used to Design Packaging...

1) You can use CAD to draw <u>nets</u> and then you can <u>manipulate</u> (alter) the design until it's right.

2) You can make your design <u>bigger</u> or <u>smaller</u>, while keeping the <u>proportions</u> the <u>same</u>.

3) You can also <u>rotate</u> your drawing or make <u>mirror images</u> of bits of it. This can help you make <u>complicated designs quickly</u>.

4) In <u>batch production</u>, lots of the <u>same nets</u> are needed. To <u>reduce waste</u> you can <u>copy and paste</u> your net loads of times onto one sheet, fitting them together as closely as possible (see page 77). <u>CAD</u> makes this <u>really easy</u>.

There's more about CAD on p.62.

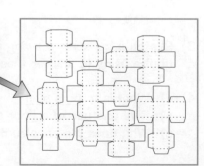

Net yourself some marks — draw a surface development...

Don't worry if you're thrown by all this talk of <u>CAD</u> and <u>CAM</u> — it's explained in more detail in <u>section 6</u>. You can use CAD to design nets in your <u>project</u> — so if it's there, then you might as well <u>have a go</u>.

Nets and Packaging

...and CAM Can be Used to Manufacture it

1) <u>CAM</u> stands for <u>Computer Aided Manufacture</u>.

2) Once you've drawn your net using CAD, you can use a <u>CAM machine</u> like a <u>vinyl cutter</u> or a <u>die cutter</u> (see below) to cut it out.

3) The CAD software works out the <u>coordinates</u> of each point on your drawing. A CAM machine can <u>follow</u> these coordinates and move the tools to <u>cut</u> out your design.

4) Using CAM to cut out your nets is <u>more accurate</u> and <u>faster</u> than doing it by hand — and you can cut out <u>lots</u> that are all the <u>same</u>.

DIE CUTTER

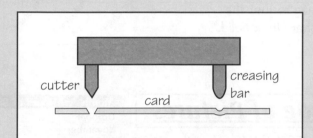

- A die cutter <u>presses out</u> the net from the sheet of material, using a sharp blade <u>specially shaped</u> to the outline of the net.

- <u>Creases</u> can be made (along the lines where the packaging will be folded) by rounded <u>creasing bars</u>.

- You have to make a blade especially to match your net, so die cutting is <u>expensive</u>, but it's great for making <u>large quantities</u> of nets with <u>complicated designs</u>.

Practice Questions

EXAM TIP
You might be asked about 'surface developments' — don't forget that these are just nets.

1) a) What is a <u>net</u>?
   b) What's another name for a net?
   c) Who's Annette?

2) Describe how nets can be useful in the <u>design</u> process.

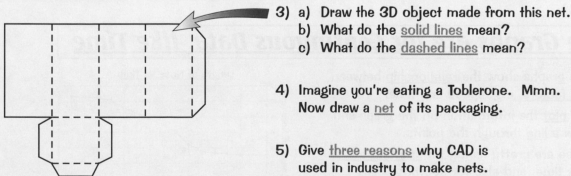

3) a) Draw the 3D object made from this net.
   b) What do the <u>solid lines</u> mean?
   c) What do the <u>dashed lines</u> mean?

4) Imagine you're eating a Toblerone. Mmm. Now draw a <u>net</u> of its packaging.

5) Give <u>three reasons</u> why CAD is used in industry to make nets.

6) Chris is using <u>CAM</u> to cut out his nets. He is using a <u>die cutter</u>.
   a) What does CAM stand for?
   b) Outline how a <u>die cutter</u> works.
   c) Explain a <u>disadvantage</u> of using a die cutter.

Charts and Graphs

Graphs and charts can show information so that it's <u>easy to understand</u>. You can use ICT — e.g. put the data from your market research into a <u>spreadsheet</u> and use that to draw a chart or graph. Then it'll be really neat — plus you can update it quickly if necessary (if you manage to collect some more data, say).

Bar Charts use Bars to Show Numbers

1) A bar chart should have <u>equally spaced</u> bars of the <u>same width</u>.

2) The bars can be drawn <u>horizontally</u> or <u>vertically</u>.

3) It's <u>easy</u> to <u>compare results</u> using a bar chart — this one shows that <u>more people</u> like <u>pictographs</u> best than like bar charts or pie charts best.

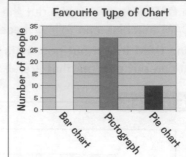

4) Data can also be displayed in <u>3D bar charts</u>. They're just the same, except the bars look solid.

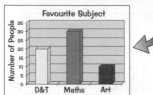

Pictographs are Charts Made of Pictures

1) Pictographs (aka <u>pictograms</u>) use <u>symbols</u> or simple <u>pictures</u> — they can make slightly <u>dull</u> information look a little bit <u>more interesting</u>.

2) They must have a <u>key</u> to show what the symbol means.

Month	Hours of Sunshine
October	☼ ☼ ☼ ☼
November	☼ ☼ ☼
December	☼ ☼
January	☼ ☼ ☼
February	☼ ☼ ☼
March	☼ ☼ ☼ ☼ ☼

☼ represents 2 hours of sunshine per day

Pie Charts Show Proportions

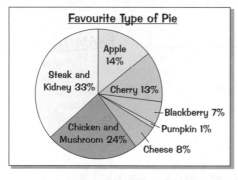

Favourite Type of Pie

Apple 14%
Steak and Kidney 33%
Cherry 13%
Blackberry 7%
Pumpkin 1%
Chicken and Mushroom 24%
Cheese 8%

1) Pie charts make it really easy to <u>compare</u> the sizes of different categories.

2) You might want to show the <u>percentage</u> for each category. (Check that the whole pie adds up to 100%.)

3) You can also draw pie charts in <u>3D</u>.

EXAM TIP
If you're asked to draw a graph or chart, don't forget to <u>label</u> it and add the <u>units</u>.

Line Graphs are for Continuous Data, like Time

1) Line graphs show the <u>relationship</u> between <u>two factors</u>, e.g. speed and time.

2) You <u>plot</u> the information on the graph and draw a <u>line</u> through the points.

3) These are pretty handy for <u>spotting trends over time</u>, and also for spotting "<u>blips</u>".

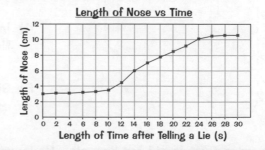

Length of Nose vs Time

And now for this week's Top 40 Charts — at number 39, Pie...

They say you're never more than 3 metres from a maths question. Still, at least this lot isn't too bad. And it's more than half a pie likely to come up in the <u>exam</u> — so you'd better get on and learn it well.

Charts and Graphs

Charts and diagrams can be used to show the <u>order</u> something is done in. Super.

A Flow Chart Shows Events in the Order they Happen

1) A <u>flow chart</u> is a diagram which shows a number of <u>events</u> in the <u>order</u> that they take place.

2) They're used when making graphic products to show the <u>order of jobs</u> during <u>manufacture</u>.

3) Flow charts have <u>feedback loops</u>, which are used for <u>quality control</u> during manufacture.

4) The feedback loops show you how to <u>fix a problem</u> if something isn't right.

For example, if the paint job isn't accurate, you know you need to <u>go back a few steps</u> and do it again.

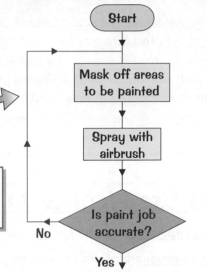

See page 13 for more on flow charts.

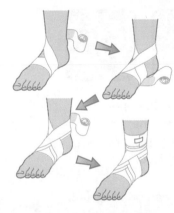

Sequential Illustrations Do the Same

1) Instead of producing a flow chart, you can use a <u>series of illustrations</u> to show how to do something.

2) You'll see examples of this when you buy <u>flat-pack</u> furniture — it comes with step-by-step <u>instructions</u> that show how to build it.

3) These instructions use <u>pictures</u> and very <u>few words</u> so that everybody should be able to follow them.

Practice Questions

1) What's the main difference between a <u>bar chart</u> and a <u>pictograph</u>?

2) What <u>percentage</u> does a full pie add up to when you draw a pie chart?

3) a) What is a <u>flow chart</u>?
   b) What are the <u>feedback loops</u> in flow charts used for?

4) a) What is a <u>sequential illustration</u>?
   b) Give an example of something you'd buy that might come with <u>sequential illustrations</u>.

5) 25 examiners were asked to name their favourite hobby — here are the results:

Hobby	Number of Examiners
Writing questions	12
Swotting up	9
Giving marks	3
Sleeping	1

a) Plot it all in a lovely <u>bar chart</u>.
b) Now show the information in a <u>pictograph</u>.
c) And why not put it in a <u>pie chart</u> too?
d) Which of your graphs and charts do you think shows the data the <u>best</u>? Explain your answer.
e) Why isn't a <u>line graph</u> a suitable graph for this data?

Signs and Labels

"A picture's worth a thousand words", or so they say — worth bearing that in mind...

Iconic Labels — Simple and Easily Recognised

1) Examples of iconic labels (or icons) appear on your computer screen as shortcuts to software, files or program tools.

2) Icons that identify functions (e.g. the text tool or the print symbol) are similar in all software packages, to help a user to quickly learn how to use new software.

3) Icons are usually small and immediately recognisable to the user.

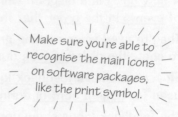
Make sure you're able to recognise the main icons on software packages, like the print symbol.

Ideograms Use Pictures to Represent Objects and Ideas

1) Ideograms (or pictograms) can be substituted for writing — they're kind of a universal language.

2) They're simplified images that are immediately identifiable.

3) You'll have seen plenty of ideograms in everyday life. E.g. if you go on holiday, you might see a sign with an aeroplane to identify an airport, or one with a telephone receiver pointing to a payphone.

4) Ideograms are sometimes used to show how to operate a product. For example, the control buttons on a stereo or MP3 player are pretty much universally recognised.

5) This recycling symbol means that some (or all) of the product can be recycled.

Symbols can be Created for Any Object

If an ideogram doesn't already exist for an object, you can create one — just follow these rules.

1) Simplify the object — just show the main features.

2) Don't use any words — then it can be used in any country.

3) Make sure the symbol is able to be reproduced if it's going to be used on a number of items.

4) Make sure it's an appropriate colour.

EXAM TIP
You might get asked to design a symbol or ideogram in your exam.

There are some standard colouring conventions that are worth considering — such as:

1) Red for STOP or warning

2) Green for GO or OK or for something environmentally friendly or vegetarian

Take it as a sign — you need to get this lot learnt...

There's a fair old bit to learn here, but you do need to know it. When you're designing a sign or label of your own, the most important thing is to make it really, really clear and dead easy to understand.

Signs and Labels

Labels can Give Product Information

1) Some labels are used to show that products have met <u>standards</u> for safety or quality, e.g. the '<u>CE</u>' mark and the <u>British Standards Kitemark</u> (see page 59).

2) There might also be information about how to <u>store</u> or <u>maintain the product</u>, or specific <u>safety</u> warnings.

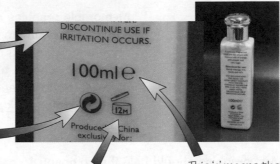

DISCONTINUE USE IF
IRRITATION OCCURS.

100ml℮

3) Many products carry <u>symbols</u> that have an <u>agreed meaning</u> throughout Europe.

This shows that the manufacturer has paid a fee to cover collection and possible recycling of the packaging.

This means that once you've opened the bottle you should <u>use the lotion up</u> within <u>12 months</u>.

This 'e' means that the <u>average bottle from the batch</u> contains <u>at least 100 ml</u> of lotion.

Food Packaging Has Lots of Symbols

Pre-packed food has to show certain information <u>by law</u> — including the ingredients list and the weight or volume. But producers often add other symbols too, for example:

Symbols are used to show that food is <u>suitable</u> for a <u>particular diet</u>, e.g. food suitable for vegetarians is often shown with a green **V**.

<u>Warnings</u> can be given of possible <u>allergy problems</u>, e.g. 'may contain traces of nuts'.

Barcodes Identify the Product

In many shops each product has a <u>unique</u> barcode. Barcodes can be read by a <u>scanner</u>.

1) <u>Scanning the barcode in</u> at the till brings up the product's <u>name and price</u>.

2) This <u>records sales</u> and so helps to <u>control stock levels</u> and <u>re-ordering</u>.

3) The information obtained about sales can also be used for <u>marketing purposes</u>.

5 000143 057629

Practice Questions

1) What are <u>iconic labels</u>? Suggest where they might be found.

2) What do you call pictures that are used to <u>represent</u> objects and ideas?

3) a) Give two symbols that might be displayed on a product's label to show that it is <u>safe</u>.
   b) Suggest another symbol you might find on a product label.

4) Describe two symbols that might be found on <u>food packaging</u>.

5) Jonny has just bought a new stereo.
   a) Draw the <u>ideogram</u> that might be on the "pause" button.
   b) <u>Design</u> an ideogram that tells the user to <u>keep the stereo out of direct sunlight</u>.

Branding and Social Responsibility

Most companies want to have a <u>strong corporate identity</u> — so consumers know what the company does. They also want consumers to feel <u>positive</u> about the company, so their products mustn't offend people.

Strong Corporate Identity Includes Brand Recognition

1) <u>Memorable graphics</u> are a really good way to make sure that consumers <u>recognise</u> your products, e.g. using a <u>logo</u>. Many companies often apply their logo and colour scheme to all <u>printed material</u> (e.g. business cards, letterheads and compliments slips) as well as their <u>products</u>, <u>packaging</u>, <u>uniforms</u> and <u>transport</u>.

2) <u>Well designed</u> graphics should help the company to get its message across, or build up its <u>corporate identity</u> — the image it wants people to have of the company.

For example, a company that wants people to think of it as modern and creative would use very different <u>colours</u> and <u>typefaces</u> from a company that wants its corporate identity to be all about tradition.

John's newspaper company was so modern that it had taken to printing the news for the whole world to see.

3) Companies like McDonald's and NIKE have <u>strong branding</u>. Many people can recognise each company from its logo alone, <u>without the need for words</u>. This is great for the company.

EXAM TIP
You might have to explain why a particular logo is good (or bad).

Companies Need To Think About Moral Implications

Many companies want to create an image of being <u>morally responsible</u>. They can do this by showing that they've <u>thought</u> about the <u>materials</u> and <u>processes</u> used to make their products. For example, they can consider:

1) whether <u>using the product</u> might <u>harm</u> people or the environment — e.g. they might try to avoid using paints and varnishes that are <u>toxic</u>.

2) whether the <u>manufacture</u> of the product <u>harms people</u>, e.g. through dangerous <u>working conditions</u>, or because components are produced using <u>child labour</u>.

3) whether the <u>manufacture</u> of the product <u>harms the environment</u>, e.g. by using up resources or producing a lot of <u>waste material</u> which the customer will need to dispose of.

4) whether <u>recycled materials</u> could be used to manufacture the product or its packaging.

5) whether <u>biodegradable or recyclable</u> materials could be used, especially if the product's designed to be <u>thrown away</u> after use.

Look, it's Russell — ooh, and there's Jo...

Successful companies often have a really recognisable logo. And they plaster it all over their products, packaging and advertisements, and on any printed material — so that people just can't ignore it.

Branding and Social Responsibility

Designers Must Be Aware of the Feelings of Others

Designers need to be <u>sensitive</u> to the feelings of different groups in society.

1) They need to make sure that designs do not <u>put off</u>, <u>insult</u> or <u>offend</u> people for <u>political</u>, <u>religious</u>, <u>gender</u> or <u>cultural</u> reasons.

2) Certain <u>symbols</u> are almost certain to offend some people no matter how they're used, e.g. a swastika.

3) Other symbolism will offend people if they believe it's been <u>misused</u> or <u>abused</u>. This is especially true for religious symbols.

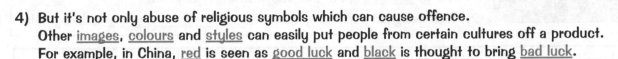

4) But it's not only abuse of religious symbols which can cause offence. Other <u>images</u>, <u>colours</u> and <u>styles</u> can easily put people from certain cultures off a product. For example, in China, <u>red</u> is seen as <u>good luck</u> and <u>black</u> is thought to bring <u>bad luck</u>.

Carol's Comics
— so simple, even a <u>woman</u> can understand them.

This sort of thing might have appeared in the 1920s...

...but you mightn't get away with it today.

5) <u>Sexism</u> and <u>racism</u>, either in text or in images, is sure to offend loads of people.

6) Some people are offended by images containing <u>nudity</u> and <u>violence</u>.

7) It's impossible to list <u>everything</u> that could cause <u>someone</u>, <u>somewhere</u> offence. Designers just have to try and put themselves in other people's shoes, and <u>imagine</u> how they might feel when they see the design.

Practice Questions

Alex's Coffee

1) Alex employed a graphic designer to come up with this <u>logo</u> for his coffee shop.
   a) Why do companies often use a logo?
   b) In what ways is the logo effective?

2) The company 'Creative Calendars' is trying to build up its <u>corporate identity</u>.
   a) What is meant by 'corporate identity'?
   b) The company likes to use <u>modern</u>, <u>colourful</u> styles in its designs. Design a <u>logo</u> for the company that shows this.

3) A company wants to create an image of being <u>morally responsible</u>.
   a) How could they make sure that they use <u>materials</u> in a responsible way?
   b) Why might they need to change the way that they <u>manufacture</u> products?

4) A swimwear company put an advert in the local paper to advertise that they are having a sale. Why might the advert <u>upset</u> some people or <u>put them off</u> buying from this company?

Summer Sale
Up to 30% off
swimwear!

Section 5 — Society and the Environment

Packaging and Sustainability

Most products come in <u>packaging</u> and it's not just there to make the product look nice. Read and enjoy...

Packaging has Loads of Functions

Protection during transport

1) When products are <u>transported</u>, they need to be protected to stop them getting <u>broken</u>.
2) Packaging materials like <u>cardboard</u> and <u>expanded polystyrene</u> can protect a product from knocks.

Storage

1) Products are often stored in <u>warehouses</u> before being put on the shop shelves. In both warehouses and shops, products are often stored <u>on top</u> of each other. The packaging has to be strong enough not to <u>collapse</u> under the weight of other objects.
2) Well designed packaging makes things <u>fit neatly together</u> side-by-side.

Display

1) Shops like to display products so that customers can <u>easily find</u> what they want.
2) Packaging is designed to make it clear <u>what the product</u> is (e.g. by using transparent windows), and also to <u>entice</u> people to buy it.
3) Companies need to be creative when designing their packaging so that their products <u>stand out</u> from the others. This could be done by using <u>bright colours</u> or a large logo.

Security

1) Packaging is also used for the <u>security</u> of the product it contains.
2) Electrical equipment such as DVDs, video games, cameras, etc. have <u>anti-theft devices</u> inserted into the packaging — this sets off an alarm if anyone tries to steal them.
3) Some security devices are filled with <u>ink</u> — if you try to take them off without the proper machine, they break open and the item is <u>ruined</u>.
4) Many food products have <u>tamper-evident seals</u> to show whether they've been <u>opened</u>.

Product information

1) When companies sell their products, they have to provide the consumers with certain <u>information</u>. For example, pre-packed food products have to list <u>ingredients</u>, the <u>best-before date</u> and various other bits of information.
2) The packaging will often also have a <u>bar code</u>, <u>customer service contact details</u>, and things like <u>storage</u> and <u>use instructions</u>.

Nobody tampered when Simon was about.

Packaging has Costs Too

All of the useful functions of packaging have meant that more and more is being used. However...

1) Packaging adds to the <u>final cost</u> of a product — the more materials used, the more expensive the product will be.
2) Also, the problem of <u>disposing</u> of the extra material is passed on to the <u>consumer</u>.
3) Packaging has a big <u>environmental impact</u> — see next page.
4) So, some <u>consumers</u> are <u>put off</u> buying things if they feel there is too much packaging used.

Avoid unnecessary waste — eat this book once you've read it...

If you thought that packaging was just for your little brother to make fantastic robot costumes, sorry. However impressive the costume, the examiner is only likely to be interested in the stuff on these pages.

Packaging and Sustainability

Graphic Products Have an Environmental Impact

Making and packaging products uses up <u>materials</u> and <u>energy</u> and produces <u>waste</u>. And many products are <u>disposed</u> of in <u>landfill</u> once they're finished with — a lot of these <u>aren't biodegradable</u> (won't rot away).

1) Products and their packaging are often made of <u>plastic</u>. Most plastic is made using <u>crude oil</u>, which is a <u>finite resource</u> (it'll run out eventually).

2) Many companies have tried to <u>reduce</u> the amount of <u>packaging</u> they use (see below). However, they still have to make sure that items are <u>protected</u>.

3) Companies also try to use <u>sustainable</u> materials. For example, products carrying the logo of the <u>Forest Stewardship Council</u> have been made using timber from <u>well managed forests</u>. 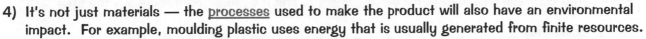 FSC

4) It's not just materials — the <u>processes</u> used to make the product will also have an environmental impact. For example, moulding plastic uses energy that is usually generated from finite resources.

Avoid Unnecessary Waste with the 6 Rs

There are things that the <u>public</u> and <u>industry</u> can do to help <u>lessen</u> the environmental impact of products.

<u>REDUCE</u> — using materials <u>economically</u>, e.g. designing the nets for packaging so that they <u>tessellate</u> means that less material is wasted (see p.77). It's also a good idea to <u>avoid unnecessary packaging</u>, e.g. by selling chocolates in a <u>paper bag</u> rather than a plastic tray in a cardboard box wrapped in cellophane.

<u>RE-USE</u> — plastic bags can be <u>re-used</u> many times. However, re-using can have an environmental impact if products need <u>transporting</u> and <u>cleaning</u> before they can be re-used.

<u>RECYCLE</u> — recycling materials means they can be used again to make new products. This helps to <u>save resources</u>, e.g. less wood is needed to make new paper and less oil is needed to make new plastic. However, it can be more <u>expensive</u> to recycle old materials than to use new ones, and environmentally unfriendly <u>by-products</u> can be produced in the process.

<u>REFUSE</u> — e.g. consumers can refuse to buy a product if they think there's <u>too much</u> packaging.

<u>RE-THINK</u> — <u>consumers</u> can think about whether they need to <u>replace</u> items so <u>often</u>, e.g. whether they need to upgrade their mobile phone each year. <u>Designers</u> can re-think their designs — they might be able to use <u>fewer parts</u> or use a less harmful <u>production process</u>.

<u>REPAIR</u> — many broken items can be <u>repaired</u> rather than fully <u>replaced</u>. For example, a radio could be fixed rather than being thrown away.

Practice Questions

1) Outline the functions of packaging <u>before</u> a product reaches the shop shelves.

2) Explain how <u>well-designed</u> packaging could increase the <u>sales</u> of a product.

3) Briefly describe two <u>impacts</u> of the increased use of packaging.

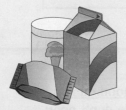

4) A company that makes food packaging is trying to improve its impact on the environment by thinking about the <u>6 Rs</u>. Outline how they could:
   a) reduce
   b) re-think

5) Give one advantage and one disadvantage of <u>re-using</u> products.

Legal Issues and Standards

Designers Can Stop People Stealing Their Ideas

Designers can stop competitors stealing their work in a number of ways:

1) **Copyright law** protects written, drawn and recorded work, e.g. books, comics, art, music and radio broadcasts. Copyright is shown by the © symbol. It runs out after a certain length of time — for books, it's 70 years after the author's death (in the UK).

2) **Registered design** protects a new design's shape and appearance, e.g. a car body shape or the design of a mobile phone casing. This stops other people from copying the design. You can register a design for up to 25 years, and it's protected throughout the EU.

3) **Trademarks** are the symbols, logos, words or slogans that are used to represent companies — other companies can't copy them. Trademarks are shown by a ™ mark after the logo, e.g. Google™. Registered trademarks are shown by an ®, e.g. Microsoft®. (Even colours can be trademarks, e.g. the particular turquoise on tins of Heinz baked beans is a trademark.)

4) **Patents** protect a new invention that could have an 'industrial application' (you won't get a patent for a nice painting you've done). Only the designer has the right to have the product manufactured, unless they sell the patent. Patents last for up to 20 years. Patents have been granted for things such as cat's eyes on roads and the humble paperclip.

So, imagine you've designed an MP3 player called the "Broccoli p-pod". You can protect:
- the appearance of the product with registered design,
- the new finger-power technology with a patent,
- the Broccoli logo with a trademark, and
- the instruction booklet and the poster used to promote it by copyright.

Other Laws Protect Consumers...

It's not just your design that you need to protect. You've got to protect the people who are going to be buying your products. If they're not careful, manufacturers who produce unsafe or unreliable products can be prosecuted under one or more of these laws.

1) The Consumer Protection From Unfair Trading Regulations ensure that any claims made about a product (e.g. that it is hard-wearing, long-lasting, waterproof) must be true.

2) The General Product Safety Regulations state that nobody can put a product on the market unless it's safe.

3) The Sale Of Goods Act ensures that products perform as you would reasonably expect and that goods last a reasonable length of time.

4) Fire Safety Regulations cover upholstered furniture and cushions, etc. to ensure that they don't catch fire easily and don't give off really toxic fumes when they burn.

Laws — always something to stop the fun...

So, when you're designing and making a product, you've got to make sure that it's good quality and that it doesn't harm your workers or customers. And you've got to make sure people don't copy it.

Legal Issues and Standards

...and Workers

There are also regulations to protect your <u>workers</u>.

> <u>COSHH</u> stands for the <u>Control of Substances Hazardous to Health</u>. These regulations were introduced in <u>1988</u> to protect people from the effects of <u>hazardous substances</u>, <u>materials</u> and <u>processes</u>.

Products are Labelled if they Meet Certain Standards

1) There are various organisations that <u>set standards</u> for certain types of product. These standards are usually about <u>safety</u> and the <u>quality</u> of <u>design</u>.

2) Products that meet these standards can usually be <u>labelled</u> to show this.

3) If a company's products meet these standards they might be more profitable — many <u>consumers</u> are more willing to buy '<u>approved</u>' products, or will <u>pay more</u> for them.

The <u>British Standards Institution (BSI)</u> is one example of a standard writing organisation. BSI independently tests products to make sure they meet British, European or International standards. For certain products (such as glass, windows or plastic pipes) a Kitemark can be awarded.

Certain types of product must also meet <u>EU standards</u> for safety, shown by the '<u>CE</u>' mark, before they can be sold in most European countries.

This logo shows that a <u>toy</u> has been made by a member of the <u>British Toy and Hobby Association</u> who agrees to stick to strict safety, marketing and ethical guidelines.

The <u>International Organisation for Standardisation</u> (<u>ISO</u>) also issues <u>certificates</u> to organisations that meet international standards of quality.

Practice Questions

1) What can <u>copyright</u> law be used to protect?

2) What is a <u>trademark</u>?

3) Pierre has designed a toaster.
   a) How can he protect the <u>shape</u> and <u>appearance</u> of the design?
   b) How long will this protection last?

4) What kinds of products could be awarded a <u>patent</u>?

5) Katie has bought a tent that <u>isn't</u> waterproof. Suggest what <u>law</u> might have been <u>broken</u>, and explain your answer.

6) What does <u>COSHH</u> stand for? What does it mean?

 7) a) What is the name of the symbol on the left?
   b) What does it mean if a product is labelled with this symbol?

8) What does the '<u>CE</u>' mark show?

Health and Safety

You need to watch out for yourself when you're working — and everyone else too.

Employers have to Provide Safe Working Conditions

1) The Health and Safety at Work Act was passed to make sure employers provide a safe working environment, and that they use safety signs to help reduce the risk of accidents.

2) It's the law that employers and workers must use safe working practices at all times.

3) Factory safety inspectors are employed to examine and investigate workplaces to check that rules and regulations are being followed.

Safety Advice Should be Followed

A lot of this is common sense. But it's incredibly important, so pay attention...

Wear Appropriate Clothing

1) While working (especially with machine tools) make sure your sleeves are rolled back, your tie and apron strings are tucked in and if you've got long hair, it's tied back.

2) Protect yourself from hazardous materials by wearing strong protective gloves and goggles.

Care Should be Taken with Tools and Machinery

1) Always use a safety rule and cutting mat when using knives.

2) Always secure work safely — e.g. clamp work securely before cutting.

3) Know how to switch off and isolate machines in an emergency.

4) Never adjust a machine unless you've switched it off and isolated it.

5) Never leave machines unattended while they're switched on.

6) Don't use machines or hand tools unless you've been shown how.

7) If dust is a danger, e.g. when you're machining board, make sure there's adequate ventilation and that dust extraction equipment is working.

8) Carry tools safely.

Handle Materials and Waste Sensibly

1) Make sure materials are safe to handle — sand down rough or sharp edges on board or plastic.

2) Lots of varnishes and glues (e.g. acrylic cement) give off harmful fumes. So make sure there's good ventilation.

3) Beware of red-hot heating elements (e.g. on hot wire cutters) and naked flames — and keep them away from flammable substances, e.g. aerosol adhesives.

4) Make sure you dispose of waste properly — this is also an environmental issue.

5) When storing material, make sure it's put away safely so it can't fall and injure anyone.

6) Never clear away sawdust with your bare hands — use a brush.

Health and safety — it's all an act...

Factories can be dangerous places and employers have to assess the risks. But school workshops can be just as dangerous — the safety advice on this page should be followed wherever you're working.

Health and Safety

Risk Assessments Should be Carried Out

1) A <u>risk assessment</u> is an <u>evaluation</u> carried out by an employer to <u>identify</u> and <u>minimise</u> any potential risks at work. A risk assessment has to be carried out when any <u>new project</u> is being planned.

2) Risk assessments are especially important wherever <u>chemicals</u> or <u>machinery</u> are being used.

3) When you're writing a risk assessment think:

> 1) What could be a <u>hazard</u>?
> 2) What <u>precautions</u> could I take to make sure the risk is minimised?

Risk assessment for project

Hazard	How to reduce the risk
Clothing could get caught in the sanding machine.	Tuck clothes in and wear an apron.
Fine dust created when using a sanding machine.	Wear a mask and use a dust extractor.
Fingers could be cut when using a craft knife.	Use a safety rule to protect fingers.

4) Many hazards present an <u>immediate, obvious risk</u>, e.g. working with sharp tools.

5) Others aren't so obvious. For example, using CAD software is usually pretty safe but if you stare at the screen for <u>long periods</u> of time without having a break you could get a <u>headache</u> (and a <u>sore back</u> as well if you sit in an uncomfortable chair to do it).

EXAM TIP
This kind of thing is a popular exam question.

Practice Questions

1) a) What is the main purpose of the <u>Health and Safety at Work Act</u>?
   b) What do <u>factory safety inspectors</u> do?

2) Dan is cutting some <u>thick card</u> down to size with a metal-cased knife. Give some safety precautions that he should follow.

3) What precaution should be taken when using varnishes that give off <u>harmful fumes</u>?

4) Laura is using a <u>hot wire cutter</u>. Give some safety precautions that she should follow.

5) Dave is planning a project and needs to write a <u>risk assessment</u>.
   a) What is a risk assessment?
   b) The project will involve cutting MDF with a fret saw. Write a risk assessment to cover the possible hazards of this process.

CAD/CAM

So, here's a spot of <u>Computer Aided Design</u> and <u>Computer Aided Manufacture</u>, or CAD/CAM to its friends.

CAD is Designing Using a Computer...

EXAM TIP
You might have to explain how CAD/CAM could be used to design and make a product.

1) Computer Aided Design (CAD) involves <u>designing products</u> on a <u>computer</u>, rather than using the traditional methods on paper.

2) CAD packages include <u>2D drawing programs</u> (e.g. TechSoft 2D DESIGN) and <u>3D modelling software</u> (e.g. Pro/DESKTOP®, Pro/ENGINEER® or SolidWorks®).

3) CAD helps designers <u>model</u> and <u>change</u> their designs quickly. It's easy to experiment with alternative <u>colours</u> and <u>forms</u> and you can spot problems <u>before making</u> anything.

4) In 3D programs, you can view the product from <u>all angles</u>.

...and CAM is Making Using a Computer

1) <u>CAM</u> is the process of <u>manufacturing</u> products with the help of <u>computers</u>.

2) CAD/CAM means linking CAD and CAM together...

3) The software uses <u>numbers</u> to represent each point on your CAD drawing. These are the <u>x,y,z coordinates</u> — x is the left/right position, y is forwards/backwards and z is up/down.

4) CAM machines are computer numerically controlled (CNC). Their onboard processor 'reads' the numerical information (the x,y,z coordinates) from the CAD design — and uses these numbers to move the tools to the correct positions to cut out or build up your design.

5) Some <u>milling machines</u> are CAM machines. They <u>remove</u> material from a larger piece of material to shape and create a product.

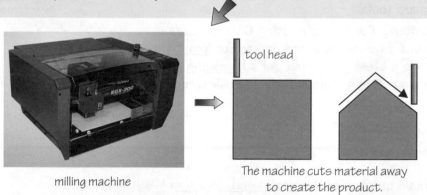

milling machine

tool head

The machine cuts material away to create the product.

6) Other examples of CAM machines are <u>CNC routers</u>, <u>laser cutters</u> and <u>laser printers</u>.

- CAD/CAM is useful when you need to produce a <u>batch</u> of products.
- You can draw your design once in CAD and then <u>copy and paste</u> the image so that the CAM machine will cut out more than one shape from your material at a time.

CAD/CAM — for telling tools where to go...

Spend a bit of time getting your head round what <u>CAD</u> and <u>CAM</u> are, and make sure you know a few <u>examples</u> of CAD software and CAM machines. Then there are the <u>pros</u> and <u>cons</u> to come next...

CAD/CAM

Using CAD/CAM has Loads of Benefits...

It's very <u>expensive</u> to <u>buy</u> and <u>set up</u> CAD/CAM systems, but it can <u>save money</u> in the <u>long run</u>. CAD/CAM has loads of <u>benefits</u> for designers and manufacturers in many different <u>industries</u>:

1) It's easy to <u>develop</u> and <u>edit</u> 2D and 3D images of your design ideas and view them from all angles. You can <u>experiment</u> with different materials and finishes, and you can <u>make changes</u> for the client without having to redraw the design.

2) Designers can produce <u>very realistic</u> designs quickly on screen, which helps their boss or the <u>client</u> to understand what the designer is proposing. Once a design is finalised, CAD can be used to produce the <u>final presentation drawing</u> with all the finishes, as well as an <u>exploded view</u> (see page 44) of all the parts.

3) With CAM, products can be machined at <u>high speed</u> so that loads can be manufactured in a <u>short time</u>.

Car bodies are made using CAM — they're produced quickly in large quantities.

4) CAM gives a <u>high quality</u> and more <u>reliable</u> finished product — there's no human error involved.

5) You can mass-produce <u>complicated products</u>. Each part can be manufactured by a <u>different machine</u> and the parts can be assembled quickly.

6) All of this means that <u>manufacturers</u> can save lots of money because <u>labour costs</u> are <u>lower</u> — <u>machines</u> are doing almost all the work.

...But there are Some Disadvantages Too

1) The <u>initial cost</u> of <u>software</u> and <u>hardware</u> is <u>high</u>.
2) Workers need <u>expensive and lengthy training</u> in how to use CAD/CAM to produce the <u>best results</u>.
3) Work can be disrupted if the computers get a <u>virus</u> or files are <u>corrupted</u>.

Practice Questions

1) a) Give an example of a piece of <u>3D CAD software</u>.
   b) Suggest why it might be a good idea to use CAD to <u>design</u> a product.

2) a) What is <u>CAM</u>?
   b) What is meant by CAM being '<u>computer numerically controlled</u>'?

3) a) Give <u>three advantages</u> of using CAD/CAM.
   b) Give <u>two disadvantages</u> of using CAD/CAM.

4) Billy wants to make a paperweight from a block of plastic. Explain how <u>CAD/CAM</u> could be used to do this.

ICT

Information and Communication Technology — another big mouthful, so let's just call it good old ICT.

ICT is Made up of Hardware and Software

1) Computer hardware is all the stuff that's, errr... hard and that you can physically move about — like the computer monitor, keyboard and input and output devices (see below).

2) Computer software is the actual computer programmes.

3) There's software to do loads of different things:

- You can use spreadsheet software to work out production costs and time management, or to make graphs showing the results of your research (see page 50).

- Painting software is really useful for manipulating photos — you can use software such as Corel®, Paint Shop Pro® and Adobe® Photoshop®.

- If you want to create a slideshow to present your product to your client, there's software for putting together a presentation.

You Use Input Devices to Enter Data...

An input device is any piece of equipment you use to get your data onto a computer. For example:

- You can use a scanner to scan an image like a photo or a hand-drawn design, and convert it into a computer file.

- You can manipulate the image as you want — crop it, resize it, change the colours, add different effects, etc.

- You can then use the image in other pieces of software and in your product.

- Digital cameras are great for taking photos because you can download them straight onto a computer.

- Then you can zoom in, crop or enhance the photos using painting software.

- Graphics tablets are great for designing using CAD.
- You draw on them using a special pen and the image appears on the computer screen.

...and Output Devices to Print or Make Stuff

1) When you want to produce a 'hard copy' (something you can actually hold) of what's on the computer, you'll need an output device.

2) Output devices include printers, and CAM machines such as milling machines, laser cutters and vinyl cutters.

ICT and when ICT I drinks it...

ICT comes in pretty handy for Graphic Products. Modern industry would grind to a halt without it. Perhaps you could write a little "ode to ICT" poem about everything it can do. Or just learn this page.

ICT

Using ICT has its Good and Bad Points

ICT is being used more and more in <u>industry</u>.
This has both <u>pros</u> and <u>cons</u>:

EXAM TIP
You might be asked to weigh up the benefits and costs of using ICT.

PROS

1) Computers can <u>increase</u> the amount of <u>work done</u>. This makes businesses more productive and so more profitable.

2) Workers benefit if computers can do boring, <u>repetitive</u> tasks and leave them to do the interesting jobs.

3) Transferring data electronically (see below) is <u>quick</u> and <u>convenient</u>.

4) The Internet is really useful as a <u>research</u> tool — it contains <u>loads</u> of information.

CONS

1) It's <u>expensive</u> to keep investing in the latest and most efficient technology, and it takes time and money to <u>retrain</u> staff.

2) There may be <u>job losses</u> as computers replace people for some tasks, e.g. using CAD/CAM to manufacture packaging.

3) Continued use of computers can cause <u>health problems</u>, e.g. repetitive strain injury.

The Electronic Transfer of Data is Useful in Industry

1) Data can be <u>transferred electronically</u> — from one computer to another, anywhere in the world. This means that <u>designing</u> and <u>manufacturing</u> can be done in <u>different locations</u> — the designer's work can be electronically transferred to the manufacturing site.

2) <u>Electronic Data Interchange</u> (EDI) is the direct transfer of information from one computer system to another, usually via the <u>Internet</u>.

3) <u>E-mail</u> can be used to <u>quickly</u> transfer written information and attachments (e.g. designs) between different locations.

4) <u>Teleconferencing</u> allows <u>meetings</u> between workers in <u>different locations</u>. A <u>camera</u> connected to a computer is linked to the Internet (or sometimes the telephone network). <u>Voices</u> and <u>moving images</u> are relayed in <u>real time</u>.

Practice Questions

1) a) What is <u>computer hardware</u>?
   b) What's <u>software</u>?

2) Why might you use a <u>spreadsheet</u> when creating a graphic product?

3) a) What is an <u>input device</u>?
   b) What is an <u>output device</u>?

4) Mandy is fed up with her work colleagues stealing her coffee mug every morning. She decides to buy a plain mug and print her name and photo on it. Give an <u>input device</u> she could use to:
   a) transfer a drawing of her name onto the computer,
   b) get an image of herself onto the computer.

5) A graphic designer has been asked to develop a series of posters and brochures to advertise a new holiday resort. Explain how the <u>electronic transfer of data</u> is useful in developing the very best product.

Systems and Quality Control

A <u>system</u> is a collection of parts that <u>work together</u> to do a particular <u>function</u>. A little bit like a nice big mug, a tea bag, boiling water, milk and a biccie — all working together to get you through revision.

A System has an Input, a Process and an Output

Manufacturing systems can be broken down into three simple elements — <u>inputs</u>, <u>processes</u> and <u>outputs</u>.

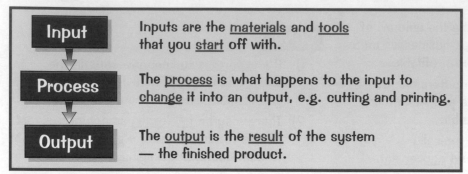

Input

Inputs are the <u>materials</u> and <u>tools</u> that you <u>start</u> off with.

Process

The <u>process</u> is what happens to the input to <u>change</u> it into an output, e.g. cutting and printing.

Output

The <u>output</u> is the <u>result</u> of the system — the finished product.

No... systems, not cisterns.

Example — photocopying

<u>Input</u>:
A4 original,
A3 paper,
toner.

<u>Process</u>:
Image
enlargement.

<u>Output</u>:
A3 copies
of the
original.

Manufacturing Systems Can be Shown on Flow Charts

1) A <u>flow chart</u> is used to show the <u>stages</u> of a manufacturing process in the <u>right order</u>.

2) <u>Feedback loops</u> in a flow chart let you <u>change the input</u> as a result of <u>quality checks</u> (see next page). For example, you can check you've got a good photograph to use before moving on to the next stage of the manufacturing process.

3) So, if your photo is too dark, you can <u>change</u> the camera settings and take another photo. You can <u>repeat</u> this until you're happy.

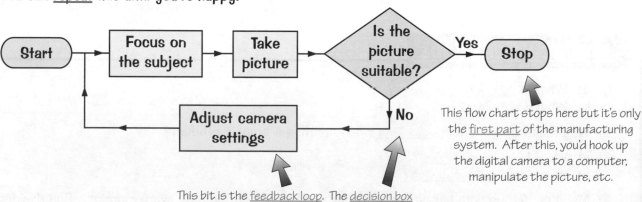

This flow chart stops here but it's only the <u>first part</u> of the manufacturing system. After this, you'd hook up the digital camera to a computer, manipulate the picture, etc.

This bit is the <u>feedback loop</u>. The <u>decision box</u> shows where the image is checked and if there's a problem, the flow chart loops back.

Input, output, shake it all about...

...you draw a graphics system and you split it down, that's what revision's all about. Whoop whoop. Not as exciting as a party song, but more important for your exam — so get learning about systems.

Systems and Quality Control

Manufacturers want <u>customer satisfaction</u> — this is achieved when a product <u>works</u>, is <u>great to use</u> and is <u>good value for money</u>. The way to make this happen is to make sure your product is <u>high quality</u>.

Quality Assurance is an Overall System

1) Quality assurance involves having good <u>staff training</u>, procedures for checking the quality of <u>materials</u> and systems for keeping <u>machinery</u> maintained.

2) It also includes <u>quality control</u> checks throughout the manufacturing process — see below.

3) So when you're planning a manufacturing system (for your project or in the exam), remember to work in <u>quality checks</u> at <u>every stage</u>. This will help your product to:

> 1) conform to the <u>manufacturing specification</u> (p.12)
> 2) do the job it's designed to do
> 3) meet the <u>standards</u> set down by the relevant institutions (p.59)
> 4) keep the <u>customer happy</u>
> 5) be manufactured <u>consistently</u>

Using templates and jigs (see page 76) and CAD/CAM helps to make sure that products are consistent.

4) Quality assurance makes sure that manufacturers don't make loads of mistakes (because they spot problems quickly) — so they won't have to do <u>recalls</u> of faulty products and refund consumers' <u>money</u>.

Quality Control Means Checking Components

Quality control means <u>testing samples</u> of components or finished products to <u>check</u> that they <u>meet</u> the manufacturing specification.

For example, a greetings card might be tested to make sure all the images are <u>printed clearly</u> (see p.74 for more on printing quality), the edges are <u>cut accurately</u>, the card is <u>folded</u> in the <u>right place</u>, the text is <u>straight</u> and it plays the <u>right tune</u>, etc.

When a component or product is checked for accuracy, it must be within a specific <u>tolerance</u>. Tolerance is given as an <u>upper</u> (+) and <u>lower</u> (−) limit for a particular measurement.

For example, you might design a card that's 200 mm tall by 120 mm wide, to fit in a slightly larger envelope. If you set a <u>tolerance of ±2.0 mm</u> then a card measuring 202 mm by 118 mm would be <u>OK</u> but a card measuring 203 mm by 120 mm would <u>not</u> be OK.

Practice Questions

1) What is a <u>system</u>?

2) What <u>three things</u> can manufacturing systems be broken down into?

3) Clive is planning his manufacturing process. Why might a <u>flow chart</u> be useful?

4) Linda is making a poster. She wants to use a guillotine to cut 50 mm off the top of a piece of paper. Draw a simple <u>flow chart</u> for this, including a <u>feedback loop</u> to show a quality check.

5) Why is it important that <u>quality checks</u> are made?

6) Derek is cropping photos to a size of 150 mm by 100 mm, with a tolerance of ±4 mm.
   a) What's the <u>smallest</u> the photos can be to be within the tolerance?
   b) What's the <u>biggest</u> the photos can be?

Scale of Production

Manufacturers use <u>different production methods</u> depending on the demand for the product they're making.

One-Off Production is Making... One Product

1) This is where you make "<u>one-of-a-kind</u>" products. <u>Every item</u> will be <u>different</u>, to meet a customer's exact requirements.

2) It's very <u>labour intensive</u> — it takes a lot of <u>time</u> to make each product. The <u>workforce</u> also needs to be <u>highly skilled</u> so it's an <u>expensive</u> way to make things.

3) One-off production is used for all sorts of things, from <u>made-to-measure furniture</u> to <u>paintings</u>.

Batch Production is Making a Set Number of Products

1) This is where you make a specific quantity of a product — called a <u>batch</u>. Batches can be <u>repeated</u> as many times as necessary.

2) Batch production is used for things like <u>leaflets</u>, <u>brochures</u> and <u>posters</u>.

3) You do <u>one process</u> on <u>the whole batch</u> then do <u>another process</u>. For example, you might <u>print</u> all of the posters first and then <u>guillotine</u> them all.

4) Batch production is used to manufacture <u>a load of one product</u> (e.g. a leaflet) then something <u>a bit different</u> (a different leaflet).

5) The <u>machinery</u> and <u>workforce</u> need to be <u>flexible</u>, so they can quickly change from making one batch to making another batch of a similar product.

6) The time <u>between batches</u>, when machines and tools may have to be set up differently or changed, is called <u>down time</u>. This <u>wastes money</u> — because you're not making anything to sell.

7) Sometimes you get a backlog of half-made products, so it's <u>not as efficient</u> as <u>mass production</u>...

Mass Production is Making Loads of the Same Product

1) This is the method you'd use to make <u>thousands</u> of <u>identical products</u>, like <u>newspapers</u> and <u>magazines</u>. You'd only use this for a <u>mass-market product</u> — where loads of people want to buy the same thing.

2) The different stages of production are <u>broken down</u> into simple <u>repetitive tasks</u>. Each worker only does a <u>small part</u> of the process, and the product moves further down an <u>assembly line</u> for each stage.

3) Mass production often uses <u>expensive specialised equipment</u> and <u>CAD/CAM</u>.

4) <u>Recruitment</u> is relatively <u>easy</u> — most of your staff don't need to be highly skilled.

Der der der der, derder-der der der — it's batch of the day...

You might be given an <u>example</u> of a product and asked what <u>method</u> you would use to manufacture it. Avoid exam pain — learn the ins and outs of these methods, and the <u>product demand</u> they meet.

Scale of Production

Continuous Production is Making Stuff Non-Stop

1) Continuous production <u>runs all the time</u>, without interruption, 24 hours a day.

2) That's because it would be too <u>expensive</u> to keep <u>stopping and restarting</u> the process, especially if certain conditions need to be kept <u>constant</u>.

3) The equipment is built to make <u>huge amounts</u> of only <u>one thing</u>. This means it's expensive but it can be designed to be <u>very efficient</u> — so the <u>cost per item</u> is <u>cheap</u>.

4) Continuous production might be suitable for, say, chocolate bar packaging — chocolate bars sell well all year round and the packaging isn't often redesigned.

Just-in-Time is Efficient but Needs Good Planning

In a <u>just-in-time</u> (JIT) system, the manufacturer gets the <u>materials</u> and <u>components</u> delivered as they're <u>needed</u> and uses them as soon as they're delivered. This has advantages:

1) It saves on space for <u>storing</u> materials — which saves <u>money</u> because you don't need to rent huge warehouses.

2) It means there's less money <u>tied up</u> in materials that aren't being used.

3) <u>Unsold</u> finished products <u>don't pile up</u>.

But it relies on <u>materials</u> and <u>components</u> being delivered <u>on time</u> and being <u>fault free</u> (because you don't have time to return faulty goods) — or else money can be lost.

An Increase in Production Changes How You Work

1) When you move from making a <u>one-off</u> product to <u>mass production</u>, it's likely you'll need to change the <u>production method</u> and the <u>order</u> that you do things in to make production as <u>efficient</u> as possible.

2) If you make a one-off product, you do <u>each process in turn</u>. But if you go into <u>mass production</u>, you'd have lots of the product on the go — different people would be working on <u>different parts</u>.

3) Manufacturers need to think about this when they're drawing up an <u>order of work</u> — they need to plan how they can work most <u>efficiently</u> and waste the least amount of money.

4) The <u>equipment</u> you use to do particular tasks will probably change too, especially if you start to <u>mass-produce</u> your product.

Practice Questions

1) Give an advantage and disadvantage of <u>one-off production</u>.

2) a) What is <u>batch production</u>?
   b) List some things made using batch production.

3) a) Why do manufacturers only mass produce items they know they'll <u>sell loads</u> of?
   b) Why is it often easier to <u>recruit staff</u> for mass production rather than for one-off production?

4) Give an example of a product made using <u>continuous production</u>.

5) a) Briefly describe what a <u>just-in-time system</u> is.
   b) Why might a manufacturer use a just-in-time system?

6) Alonzo has designed a T-shirt. It's really popular, so he decides to mass-produce it. Suggest how his production <u>method</u> might <u>change</u> when he increases production.

Packaging and Mechanisms

Looking at <u>product packaging</u> can give you lots of <u>ideas</u> for stuff you have to make yourself.

Packaging is Made in Different Ways

Vacuum Forming Sucks Air In

1) A sheet of <u>thermoplastic</u> is heated until it goes soft.

2) A mould is put onto the <u>vacuum bed</u>. The bed is then lifted <u>close</u> to the heated plastic.

3) The air is <u>sucked</u> out from under the plastic, creating a <u>vacuum</u>. The air pressure from outside the mould then forces the plastic onto the mould.

4) Vacuum forming can be used to make the rigid polystyrene trays for <u>mobile phone packaging</u>.

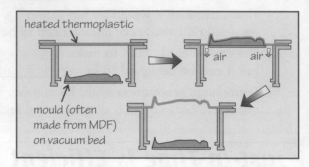

heated thermoplastic

air   air

mould (often made from MDF) on vacuum bed

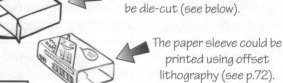

The cardboard box could then be die-cut (see below).

The paper sleeve could be printed using offset lithography (see p.72).

Blow Moulding... Well,,, Blows Air In

1) A tube of <u>softened plastic</u> is inserted into a <u>solid mould</u>.

2) <u>Air</u> is then injected which forces the plastic to <u>expand</u> to the <u>shape</u> of the <u>mould</u>.

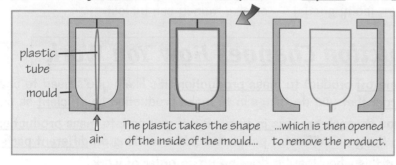

plastic tube

mould

air   The plastic takes the shape of the inside of the mould...   ...which is then opened to remove the product.

3) This method is used to produce packaging such as plastic bottles for <u>milk</u> or <u>fizzy drinks</u>.

Die Cutting is Used for Cutting and Creasing Nets

Packaging can also be made by cutting and creasing <u>nets</u> with a <u>die cutter</u> (see p.48-49). For example, some milk is packaged in waxed card cartons that are die-cut.

1) Die cutting is used to <u>cut</u> shapes out of and <u>crease</u> lines into card, paper and plastic.

2) It's used to produce the <u>nets</u> of <u>complex-shaped products</u>, e.g. packaging.

3) Making the die cutter involves bending <u>sharp blades</u> (for cutting) and <u>round-edged blades</u> (for creasing) into the right shape, so that they match the outline of the net.

4) Then they're mounted on a <u>strong plywood</u> base and <u>pressed down</u> onto the card.

5) You can cut through <u>many layers</u> of material at a time, so you can make <u>loads</u> of nets <u>very quickly</u>.

Die cutting — for when you roll a 6 but only need a 3...

Packaging can be made in lots of different ways — vacuum forming, blow moulding, die cutting... You need to know the details of each, and what kinds of products are made using what methods.

Packaging and Mechanisms

One way of making your product stand out and appeal to customers is to use <u>mechanisms</u>.

Mechanisms Create Movement

1) A pop-up is something that <u>moves</u> as you <u>open and close</u> a page.
2) Pop-ups make books and cards <u>more interesting</u> and <u>eye-catching</u> — they're often used in <u>children's books</u> and <u>novelty greetings cards</u>.
3) Mechanisms are used to create several types of <u>motion</u>.
4) A simple type of pop-up mechanism is the <u>v-fold</u> mechanism.

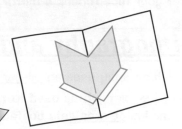

Levers, linkages and pivots make things move

1) <u>Levers</u> can be attached to the main part of the card or book, and help something to <u>move</u>.
2) You can connect levers together to form <u>linkages</u>.
3) Levers and linkages move around <u>pivots</u> to change the <u>type</u> or <u>direction</u> of motion. There are <u>four</u> different types of motion:

> <u>Linear motion</u> — moving one way in a straight line.
> <u>Reciprocating motion</u> — moving backwards and forwards in a straight line.
> <u>Oscillating motion</u> — moving backwards and forwards in an arc, e.g. a swing.
> <u>Rotary motion</u> — moving in a circle, e.g. a wheel.

4) <u>Split pins</u> are used to <u>link</u> two levers together at a pivot or to let a lever <u>rotate</u>.

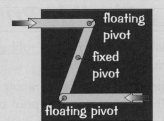

<u>Floating pivots</u> join levers together. They aren't attached to the card.

<u>Fixed pivots</u> are attached to the card and the levers rotate around these points.

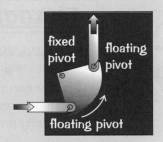

Integrated Circuits are Used to Attract Attention

1) <u>Integrated circuits</u> (ICs) or 'chips' are <u>electrical circuits</u>. They're often very <u>complicated</u> but they're incredibly <u>tiny</u>.
2) ICs are built to perform particular <u>functions</u>...
3) Products like <u>musical greetings cards</u> use ICs that play a tune as you open the card. <u>Flashing badges</u> use ICs that light up the badge when it's turned on.
4) ICs are used in products to <u>attract attention</u> and <u>improve the appearance</u>.

Practice Questions

1) Give an <u>example</u> of a product that uses vacuum formed packaging.

2) a) Briefly describe how <u>blow moulding</u> works.
   b) Give an <u>example</u> of packaging made using blow moulding.

3) Sid is making a point-of-sale display for a new computer game to go in 100 shops.
   a) Explain how he could make the cardboard display stands using <u>die cutting</u>.
   b) How could <u>integrated circuits</u> be used in the display?

Printing — Commercial Methods

I can tell you're desperate to learn all about the different <u>printing methods</u> — I can, it's written all over your face (check a mirror). So here are two pages full of fun printing facts. (Cos I'm nice like that.)

Lithography and Offset Lithography Use 'Oily' Ink

1) Lithography uses an <u>oil-based ink</u> and <u>water</u> and works on the principle that <u>oil and water don't mix</u>.

2) <u>Ultraviolet light</u> is used to transfer the image onto a smooth <u>aluminium printing plate</u> — the <u>image area</u> gets coated with a chemical that <u>attracts</u> the <u>oily ink</u> but <u>repels water</u>.

3) So the <u>image</u> area holds <u>ink</u> and the <u>non-image</u> area holds <u>water</u>.

4) In <u>offset lithography</u>, the image is printed onto a rubber '<u>blanket</u>' cylinder which squeezes away the water and transfers the ink to the paper.

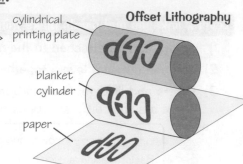

Offset Lithography

cylindrical printing plate
blanket cylinder
paper

5) Lithography and offset lithography are <u>fast</u> ways of printing and they give you a <u>high-quality</u> product.

6) They're great for print runs of <u>1000 copies or more</u> — so you can print <u>books</u>, <u>newspapers</u>, <u>magazines</u>, <u>packaging</u>, etc.

Flexography Uses a Flexible Printing Plate

1) <u>Flexography</u> uses a printing plate made of <u>flexible rubber or plastic</u>. The image <u>sticks out a bit</u> from the plate.

2) You can print onto <u>different surfaces</u> using flexography — they don't have to be completely flat either. This means you can print onto things that aren't totally smooth, like <u>cardboard</u>, or other packaging such as <u>plastic bottles</u>.

3) It's <u>quicker</u> than lithography and the printing plates <u>last for longer</u>.

4) Flexography is used for <u>large</u> print runs (over 5000) like <u>packaging</u>, <u>carrier bags</u> and <u>wallpaper</u>.

EXAM TIP
You might have to suggest a suitable printing method for a product.

Gravure Uses an Etched Printing Plate

1) Gravure uses an <u>etched</u> brass printing plate — meaning the image is <u>lower</u> than the surface of the plate and the ink fills the etched bits.

2) It's <u>expensive</u> to set up but it's <u>really fast</u> and ideal for <u>very large print runs</u> (a million copies or more). The products are <u>higher quality</u> than ones printed using lithography.

3) Gravure is used to make products such as <u>postage stamps</u>, <u>photos</u> in books and catalogues, and <u>colourful magazines</u>.

Lithography — try saying that with your mouth full of toffee...

Of course, here at CGP we still use quail feathers dipped in ink to handwrite every single page, and wax crayons to colour stuff in. But you don't need to know that — you need to learn these modern ways...

Printing — Commercial Methods

Screen Printing Uses a... Screen

1) In screen printing, a <u>stencil</u> is put under a <u>fine mesh screen</u>, and <u>ink</u> is spread over the top. The ink goes through the stencil and prints onto the material below (see p.38).

2) It's a <u>low-cost</u> process, ideal for <u>short</u> print runs of up to a few hundred copies where <u>fine detail</u> isn't needed.

3) You can use it to print onto <u>various surfaces</u> (e.g. paper, card, fabric) — so it's great for printing <u>posters</u>, <u>T-shirts</u>, <u>estate agents' signs</u>, etc.

Digital Printing Doesn't Use Printing Plates

1) Digital printing is done using <u>inkjet</u> and <u>laser</u> printers.

2) You don't have to make any printing plates, so it's <u>less fiddly</u> than many other methods.

3) There are <u>no set-up costs</u> apart from buying a printer and ink cartridges (which will need replacing when they run out).

4) Digital printing is <u>expensive</u> per sheet but for <u>short</u> print runs (hundreds of copies) it's <u>cheaper</u> than setting up the plates for another printing process, e.g. lithography.

5) It's used to print <u>posters</u>, <u>flyers</u>, <u>digital photos</u>, etc.

Practice Questions

1) How does <u>lithography</u> work?

2) Give one advantage of <u>flexography</u>.

3) What is <u>gravure</u>?

4) How does <u>screen printing</u> work?

5) a) What type of printers are used for <u>digital printing</u>?
   b) Give <u>one advantage</u> of digital printing.

6) A company wants to print thousands of <u>programmes</u> for a music concert.
   a) Suggest a suitable printing method for the company to use and explain your answer.

   The company also wants to sell merchandise at the concert. Suggest the most suitable printing methods for the following products and explain your reasons:
   b) <u>T-shirts</u> with the event logo,
   c) <u>mugs</u> with various pictures on,
   d) high-quality <u>photos</u> of the musicians.

Printing Quality and Finishes

Manufacturers use various <u>quality control marks</u> to keep an eye on the quality of printing.

Registration Marks Check the Position of the Plates

1) Printers use <u>colour registration marks</u> to check the printing plates are <u>aligned</u> in the right position.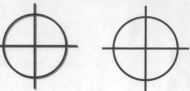
   (There are four printing plates — see page 38.)

2) If the printing plates aren't in all the right position, the image will be printed a bit <u>fuzzy</u>.

3) If the plates <u>are</u> all in the right places you get a single, clear image.

Colour Bars Check the Density of the Colours

1) <u>Colour bars</u> are printed at one edge of a sheet. They're used to check that the <u>colours</u> are being printed correctly.

2) The colour bar shows the <u>density</u> of each colour. The print worker checks these and can change the settings on the machines if any <u>fine tuning</u> is needed.

3) Without a colour bar, you wouldn't get <u>consistent colours</u> every time.

Crop Marks Show Where to Cut the Sheet

1) Printers print <u>crop marks</u> on to sheets to show where the printed sheet needs to be <u>cut to size</u> (guillotined).

2) The crop marks are printed at <u>each corner</u> and <u>dotted lines</u> show where the page should be cut — they don't show on the actual page though.

3) The sheet is printed with the background colour extending about <u>3 mm</u> beyond the crop marks — this extra bit is called the <u>bleed area</u>. This is done to ensure that there are <u>no white marks</u> around the edges of the cut sheet, even if it's cut <u>slightly too large</u>.

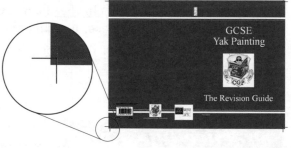

Print Finishes Can Make Your Product Look Top Quality

After the colours have been printed, you can use a <u>print finish</u> (see next page) on your product.

- Finishes can <u>improve</u> the <u>look</u> of your image. Your final product will look nice and professional — so people are more likely to <u>buy it</u>.
- They help to <u>protect</u> your product from being damaged.

...But adding a print finish can be <u>expensive</u>.

Crop marks — when you drive a tractor across a field...

When you're printing <u>loads</u> of a product, you want to make sure they all <u>look pretty darn good</u> — so manufacturers will pay a little extra to add a <u>finish</u> (see next page). Good for them — <u>now learn 'em</u>.

Printing Quality and Finishes

Varnishing Makes Things Shiny

1) Varnishing is used to make things look <u>smooth</u> and <u>glossy</u>, so they look more exciting and high-quality.

2) You can varnish the <u>whole product</u>, e.g. <u>playing cards</u> — this makes them slide over each other.

3) Or you can varnish <u>specific areas</u> (e.g. <u>book titles</u>) to draw attention to them — this is called <u>spot varnishing</u>.

Laminating Means Sandwiching in Plastic

1) Laminating means <u>sandwiching</u> a document, e.g. a menu, <u>between</u> two layers of <u>plastic</u>. The laminating machine <u>heats</u> the plastic and <u>seals</u> it together.

2) Laminating <u>business cards</u>, <u>menus</u> and <u>posters</u> makes them last longer without getting <u>damaged</u>.

3) Many <u>packaging materials</u> are a lamination of different papers, cards, plastics and aluminium foil — see p.16.

Embossing Leaves a Raised Impression

1) <u>Embossing</u> means pushing a <u>shaped die</u> into the back of the material to leave a slightly <u>raised impression</u> on its surface.

2) It's used to <u>draw attention</u> to a particular bit of the product, e.g. the <u>title</u> of a book, a <u>logo</u> or an <u>image</u>.

3) It's an <u>expensive</u> process but it adds <u>texture</u> and can suggest <u>quality</u>.

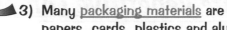

a quality Canadian number plate

Foil Application Makes Things Look Fancy

1) Foil application (or foil blocking) means using <u>heat</u> and <u>pressure</u> to <u>print metal foil</u> onto certain areas of a product.

2) Like embossing, it's used in packaging to <u>draw attention</u> to a <u>logo</u> or <u>brand name</u>, and to give the impression of a <u>quality</u> product — but it's <u>expensive</u>.

3) It's also used on <u>greetings cards</u>, <u>book titles</u> and <u>wrapping paper</u>.

Practice Questions

1) What's this, and what is it used for?

2) What's the purpose of a <u>colour bar</u>?

3) a) What are <u>crop marks</u>?
   b) What's meant by the <u>bleed area</u>?

4) How can a product be improved by:
   a) <u>varnishing</u>,   b) <u>laminating</u>,   c) <u>embossing</u>,   d) <u>foil application</u>?

Production Methods

If you were making a <u>batch</u> of products, it'd be a right pain to mark each one out with a ruler before doing the cutting. Instead, you could use a <u>template</u> to save time. <u>Jigs</u> and <u>moulds</u> also <u>speed things up</u>.

Templates are Used to Make Repetitive Shapes

1) <u>Templates</u> are used to <u>draw</u>, <u>scribe</u> or <u>cut round</u>. They're very <u>easy to make</u> and <u>simple to use</u>.

2) You can use them to <u>reproduce</u> any number of <u>identical shapes</u> from one original <u>pattern</u> (template).

3) <u>Templates</u> need to be <u>strong</u> and <u>hard-wearing</u> — so that they can be used <u>repeatedly</u> without getting damaged or worn.

4) Afterwards, the components can be <u>checked</u> against the templates for <u>accuracy</u>.

template

Jigs Help Manufacture Repetitive Components

1) A jig <u>guides</u> the <u>tools</u>, e.g. drills, that are working on a component.

2) <u>Jigs</u> come in many <u>different shapes and sizes</u> and can be <u>specifically</u> made for a particular job.

3) They're designed to <u>speed up production</u> and <u>simplify</u> the <u>making</u> process.

4) They also help cut down on <u>errors</u>, and make sure every component is <u>identical</u>.

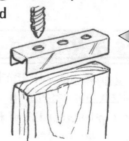

This kind of jig fits over the end of the plank and makes it <u>easy</u> to <u>drill</u> the holes in the <u>right places</u>.

EXAM TIP
You could suggest using some of these things if you're asked how to make a batch of products.

Moulds are Used to Reproduce Shapes

1) <u>Moulds</u> are most commonly used when manufacturing <u>plastic products</u> in processes such as <u>vacuum forming</u> and <u>blow moulding</u> (see p.70).

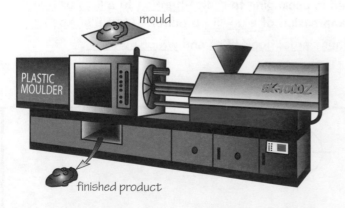

mould

PLASTIC MOULDER

SK100Z

finished product

2) Once an <u>accurate</u> mould has been made, <u>detailed</u> plastic shapes can be formed with it <u>over and over again</u>.

3) <u>Industrial moulds</u> can be <u>expensive to produce</u> (especially if they're made out of metal), so a manufacturer needs to be <u>certain</u> of the <u>design</u>. It's only cost-effective to make a mould if <u>large numbers</u> of a product are needed.

Nope — nothing about Scottish dancing here...

Templates, jigs and moulds may not sound like the best night in, but your revision will be worth it if this lot come up in the exam. Plus, you need to get your celebratory jig ready for the last page of the book.

Production Methods

Wasting Materials Means Losing Money

1) Any material that manufacturers <u>waste</u> means a <u>loss of money</u>.

2) So when they're making products, they have to make the <u>best use</u> of the materials.

3) If manufacturers can make their product for less money, it means they can afford to <u>sell</u> it to us <u>more cheaply</u> too. Bonuses all round.

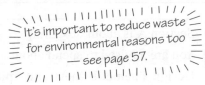
It's important to reduce waste for environmental reasons too — see page 57.

Tessellate Shapes to Reduce Waste

1) When you're making a <u>batch</u> of the <u>same product</u>, you can reduce waste by making as <u>many products</u> as possible from the <u>least amount of material</u>.

2) For example, manufacturers can try to cut as many shapes from <u>one sheet</u> of material as possible.

3) To do this they try to use shapes that <u>tessellate</u> — this means that <u>repeats</u> of the shape <u>fit together</u> without any <u>gaps</u> or <u>overlapping</u> pieces. For example, a <u>hexagon</u> shape tessellates really well.

4) It's worth playing about with an <u>odd shape</u>, like a cube net, to try and fit as many as possible on one sheet of material.

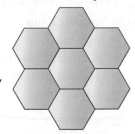
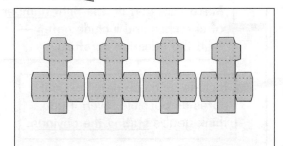
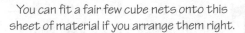
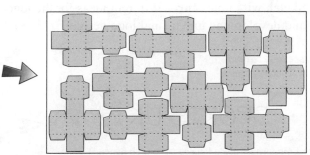

You can fit a fair few cube nets onto this sheet of material if you arrange them right.

Practice Questions

1) What are the <u>main advantages</u> of using templates, jigs and moulds?

2) Why must <u>templates</u> be hard-wearing?

3) How does a <u>jig</u> help when manufacturing repetitive components?

4) When might making a mould <u>not</u> be <u>cost effective</u>?

5) A company that manufactures signs wants to reduce the amount of material they <u>waste</u>.
   a) Give <u>two reasons</u> why it's important for manufacturers to <u>reduce waste</u>.
   b) The company is trying to reduce waste by <u>tessellating</u> the shapes that they cut out from sheets of material. Explain what this means.

Exam Technique

1) The exam lasts <u>2 hours</u>. There's <u>one paper</u> split into <u>two sections</u>.

2) <u>Section A</u> is the <u>design question</u>. <u>Section B</u> is a load of questions on anything and everything you've learned — <u>materials</u>, <u>tools</u>, <u>drawing and shading techniques</u>, etc.

Section A is the Design Question

Section A is about designing.

You are advised to spend about 35 minutes on this question.

Design Theme: Fitness and Sport

1 (a) Use the design brief and specification below to create and present a logo and apply it to the given product.

Brief

Design a promotional logo for the fitness company 'Sports UK' who are opening up a new sports centre.

Design Specification

The logo must:
- include the name 'Sports UK'
- include images related to sport and fitness
- use colour

> A bit before the exam, your teacher will give you a <u>preparation sheet</u>. This tells you what the <u>theme</u> of the design question will be. Use this to do some <u>research</u> and <u>practise</u> a few designs.

> The examiners suggest <u>how long</u> you should spend on each question — pay attention to this so you don't spend too long on one thing.

> <u>Pay attention</u> to the specification. You won't get full marks unless you cover <u>all the points</u>.

1 (a) (i) Sketch with notes **three** different ideas for the logo and develop one into a final logo design. *(13 marks)*

Letters are easy to read, especially from a distance.

Figures will be brightly coloured to draw the eye.

SPORTS UK

Stylised, modern aerobics figures tie in with fitness theme.

Tennis player links to sporting theme.

SPORTS UK

Bright red lettering to contrast with the black silhouette.

Sporting imagery

Bold, capital lettering is easy to read and makes the company name stand out.

SPORTS UK

Blue outline so the letters really leap out at you.

SPORTS UK

Will be coloured green to look like grass. This ties in with the football graphic.

Net, to tie in with football theme.

> Make sure you do the right <u>number</u> of sketches and include <u>notes</u> — read the question carefully.

> Include as much <u>detail</u> in your notes as possible, even if you think you're <u>stating the obvious</u>.

> You're just asked to sketch here — your drawings can be <u>freehand</u>. You're getting marks for how <u>interesting</u> and <u>creative</u> your ideas are.

> Make sure each design idea is <u>different</u> from the others — you won't get marks if they're too similar.

> You can add <u>colour</u> to your sketches if you like, but don't <u>spend ages</u> making them really neat — these are only supposed to be your <u>initial design ideas</u>.

> You're asked to <u>develop</u> one of your ideas into a final logo design — so show <u>how</u> you've got from the early sketches to your final idea.

Exam Technique

1 (a) (ii) Produce a coloured **presentation drawing** of your final logo design in the box below. *(6 marks)*

> This is your final drawing. You get marks for it being <u>original</u> and creative, as well as <u>neat and tidy</u>. You should use <u>colour</u> too — you won't get more than half marks if you don't.

1 (b) Sports UK want to produce a T-shirt to give away to members of the centre. A package to hold the T-shirt is required. In the space below use sketches and notes to design the package.

Marks will be awarded for:
- choice of materials used *(1 mark)*
- constructional details *(5 marks)*
- environmental considerations *(2 marks)*

> The examiner is giving you some big hints here — make sure you write or draw something to <u>cover all</u> these points fully.

> There's <u>no right or wrong answer</u> when it comes to what type of package you decide to design. You could have a plastic bag, a cardboard box, a tube...

The packaging will be a cardboard tube with a plastic lid.

Side view
— Solid end to tube

— Logo printed using flexography

— Lid pushes on at this end

Lid made from recyclable plastic, e.g. polypropylene, so new plastic doesn't need to be made using crude oil.

Lid (plan view)

Lid (side view)

Blue colour to match that in logo

> Make sure you choose <u>appropriate materials</u> (so no stainless steel in this case).

Tube made from unbleached, recycled card (bleaching chemicals harm the environment and using recycled card means fewer trees need to be cut down).

> When talking about the environmental considerations, always give an <u>explanation</u>.

Lid and tube constructed separately by different manufacturers.

Net design for tube. It will be cut out and created using a die cutter.

Constructed tube

— Fold line

Base (only one closed end is needed)

Tabs, to be glued to base using rubber-based cement

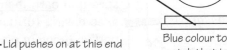

Lid will be made from polypropylene using vacuum forming.

> You get the <u>most marks</u> for saying how your packaging will be constructed, so this is the bit you need to spend the <u>most time</u> on.

> Don't forget to <u>include details</u> about how the different components will be attached together.

> It's a good idea to mention <u>specific processes</u> that could be used to make the components.

Exam Technique

Here are some of the kinds of questions you'll face in <u>Section B</u>.

Section B Covers Everything

This question is about representing data.

You are advised to spend about 7 minutes on this question.

2   A survey of the preferred font colour on a brochure gave the following results:

50 preferred blue	20 preferred yellow
30 preferred green	10 preferred red

2 (a) In the space below, draw a suitably coloured chart **or** diagram to represent this information.

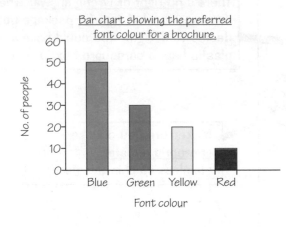

Bar chart showing the preferred font colour for a brochure.

No. of people / *Font colour*

(6 marks)

> The question says to draw a chart <u>or</u> a diagram, so <u>don't waste time</u> drawing both.

> You're asked to <u>use colour</u>, so make sure you do.

> You can represent the data any way you like — you could have drawn a <u>pictograph</u> or <u>pie chart</u> here instead.

> Make sure your diagram or chart is really <u>neat</u> — use a <u>ruler</u> for straight lines.

> There are <u>6 marks</u> here — make sure you <u>earn them</u>. <u>Label</u> your axes clearly (or use a <u>key</u> if you've drawn a pictograph) and give your chart or diagram a <u>title</u>.

This question is about sketching and equipment.

3   Items of equipment needed to make a corrugated plastic sign are shown below. Fill in the details for each item.

Item 1

Name of equipment ....metal-cased knife........

Use ...Cutting tough materials, e.g. thick board... and plastic.

Safety considerations ...Use a safety rule and... cutting mat. Keep your fingers away from the blade.

(4 marks)

> Be <u>specific</u> — say what <u>type</u> of knife it is, or you won't get the marks.

> Give as <u>full</u> an answer as possible — give <u>examples</u> of the materials it's used to cut.

> Even if you think an answer is too <u>obvious</u> to be what the examiner wants, write it down anyway — some questions will be <u>easier</u> than others. There's no point looking for a more complicated answer.

Exam Technique

This question is about materials.

4 (a) Different materials have properties which make them suitable for different uses.
Complete the table below by explaining why the material shown is suitable for the use indicated.

Material	Typical Use	Reason
Acetate	Product packaging	It's flexible and transparent so you can see the product.

(2 marks)

> This is worth two marks so give a <u>full explanation</u> — <u>don't</u> just put a one word answer.

This question is about designers and their work.

5 (a) Briefly explain why Jock Kinneir and Margaret Calvert's designs for road signs proved so popular with drivers.

The typeface uses curvy lower case letters and is clear

and easy for drivers to read when travelling at speed.

Simple pictograms are often used instead of words, which

can be distracting to read whilst driving.

These pictograms are easy to understand and are

instantly recognisable, even at a distance. The signs also

have a simple map showing the road layout ahead —

again, this is easy for drivers to understand.

(6 marks)

> You'll be asked at least one question which tests your <u>written communication</u> skills. For these questions you need to write in <u>full sentences</u> and check your <u>spelling</u> and <u>grammar</u>.

> In questions like this, the examiner is looking out for the <u>right terminology</u>, e.g. typeface and pictogram.

> There are <u>6 marks</u> up for grabs here. You need to make <u>at least 3</u> good points and <u>back them up</u> with a <u>reason</u> or <u>explanation</u>.

This question is about materials.

6 (a) A designer is mounting drawings onto a display board. Give an advantage of using spray adhesive for this use.

The glue allows for repositioning so you can move your work

around while the glue is still wet. This is good for making

displays as you might change your mind about layout.

(2 marks)

> The key phrase here is '<u>for this use</u>' — you need to make your answer <u>relevant</u> to this <u>particular situation</u>.

> When you think you've <u>finished</u> the exam, go back and <u>read over</u> your answers to check for <u>mistakes</u>. You might even think of something else you could <u>add</u>.

Glossary

adhesive	Something used to stick things together.
analyse	Study something to discover and evaluate its features.
anthropometrics	Body measurement data.
batch	A set number of identical products that are made together.
binding	Binding is used to hold sheets of paper together in the form of a book.
biodegradable	Something that will decay over time, e.g. paper. (Glass, metal and most plastics are not biodegradable.)
board	Thick paper weighing over 200 grams per square metre (200 gsm).
BSI	British Standards Institution. It sets standards for the quality and safety of products and methods. A product that meets these standards can display the Kitemark.
built-in obsolescence	When something is designed so that it becomes useless or out of date quickly.
CAD/CAM	Designing and manufacturing using a computer.
colour fusion	When tiny dots of different colours really close together blend into a new colour.
complementary	Complementary colours are found opposite each other on the colour wheel, e.g. green and red, yellow and purple, and blue and orange.
contrasting	Contrasting colours are colours that stand out against each other.
copyright	Legal protection which prevents copying of written, drawn or recorded work.
corporate identity	The image that people have of a company, e.g. its personality, style and brand.
corrugated	With a ridged or grooved surface.
crating	Drawing in 3D by starting with a box and taking bits off or adding bits on.
design brief	The instructions that the client gives to the designer about what they want the product to be like.
design specification	A list of conditions that a product should meet.
ergonomic	Easy and comfortable for people to use.

Glossary

finishes	Finishes <u>protect a product</u> from dirt and damage and <u>improve its looks</u>.
finite	A finite resource is one that will <u>run out eventually</u>, e.g. crude oil.
fixings	Fixings are used to hold different components/parts of a product <u>together</u>.
freehand	Drawing without using any <u>equipment</u> — only a pen or pencil.
gap in the market	An area where there <u>aren't any products</u> available to meet people's needs.
geometric	Geometric shapes are <u>simple, regular shapes</u> like squares and circles.
gsm	<u>Grams per square metre</u>, the way of showing the thickness of paper or board.
highlight	<u>Lighter colouring</u> used in drawings to show a surface facing the light.
horizontal	Horizontal lines run <u>left to right</u>.
hue	Another word for <u>colour</u>.
input device	Something used to <u>enter data</u> into a computer, e.g. a scanner.
laminated	<u>Covered</u> with a layer of <u>another material</u>.
manipulate	<u>Alter</u> in some way, e.g. change the colours in a CAD drawing.
manufacturing specification	A manufacturing specification tells a manufacturer exactly <u>how to make a product</u>.
market research	Asking the target market what they <u>like</u> or <u>dislike</u> about products, to help you with your design.
mock-up	A <u>full-scale model</u> made of <u>cheap materials</u> used to check the layout of a design.
model	A <u>practice version</u> of a product that you make during the development stage. It's likely to be made from easy-to-work materials and might be scaled down in size.
net	A <u>2D</u> shape that can be folded to make a 3D object. Also called a <u>surface development</u>.
output device	Something used to transfer data out of the computer, often as a '<u>hard copy</u>' or product.
patent	<u>Legal protection</u> that prevents people copying the design of a new <u>invention</u>.

Glossary

perspective drawing	Drawing in <u>3D</u>, so that things that are <u>further away</u> look <u>smaller</u>.
pictorial drawing	Drawing in <u>3D</u>.
product life-cycle	The <u>stages</u> a product goes through, from introduction to evolution or decline.
prototype	A full-size, working, one-off model of a design. A prototype is built to allow <u>evaluation</u> of the product before starting manufacturing in quantity.
registered design	<u>Legal protection</u> that prevents someone copying a design's <u>shape</u> and <u>appearance</u>.
rendering	Adding <u>shading</u> and/or <u>colour</u> to a drawing to make it look more realistic.
risk assessment	Identifying <u>potential hazards</u> and the <u>precautions</u> needed to minimise risks before work starts.
sketch	A <u>simple, freehand drawing</u>.
smart material	A material that <u>changes its properties</u> in response to a change in the environment.
sustainable	A sustainable process or material is one that can be used without causing <u>permanent damage</u> to the environment or using up <u>finite resources</u>, e.g. sustainable wood comes from forests where fast-growing trees are chopped down and replaced.
target market	The group of people who you want to <u>sell</u> your product to.
tessellation	Fitting as <u>many nets as possible</u> on to a piece of material to reduce waste.
thermochromic	Thermochromic materials <u>change colour with heat</u>.
thermoplastics	Plastics that can be <u>melted</u> and <u>re-shaped</u> over and over again.
tone	How <u>light</u> or <u>dark</u> a colour is.
trademark	<u>Legal protection</u> that prevents people copying the <u>symbols</u>, <u>logos</u> or <u>slogans</u> that represent a company.
vanishing point	A point in the distance (usually on the horizon) where <u>parallel lines</u> seem to <u>meet</u>.
vertical	Vertical lines run <u>up and down</u>.
working drawing	A <u>detailed scale drawing</u> that shows all the dimensions of each part of a product, and the materials from which components are to be made, etc.

Answers

Page 3 — Product Life-Cycle

1) A gap in the market is where there aren't products available to meet people's needs.

2) a) The group of people you're aiming to sell the product to.
   b) People with young children.

3) Introduction — a product is launched.
   Growth — sales go up, manufacturing costs go down and profits increase.
   Maturity — sales are high but there are competitors.
   The product may be reduced in price.
   Evolution — The product is changed and relaunched.
   OR Decline — The product is withdrawn from sale as sales and profits reduce.

4) a) When a product is deliberately designed so that it'll become useless quickly.
   b) E.g. use poor quality materials, e.g. low quality card. / Make the design really up to the minute, e.g. featuring celebrities.
   c) Advantage — it drives innovation / it keeps designers and manufacturers employed.
   Disadvantage — it's bad for the environment as products are thrown away / making replacement products uses up resources and energy / customers might get annoyed about having to replace the product.

5) Some products would be really expensive/inconvenient to keep replacing, so customers demand products that can be maintained.

Page 5 — Product Analysis

1) Any two from, e.g. making the lettering clear and easy to read / what colours to use / making it a suitable size.

2) a) It might help her to come up ideas for her diary. She will be able to identify good and bad features of existing products and identify ways to make her product better.
   b) (i) E.g. has a nice-looking cover, the layout of the days and weeks is easy to use.
   (ii) E.g. the printing is clear, the binding is secure.

3) a) human measurements
   b) e.g. back length, chest width, neck circumference

4) Most people don't have the average measurements so he's made sure his product will fit the majority of the target market.

Page 7 — Designers and What They Do

1) a) Harry Beck
   b) It isn't geographically correct — it shows all the lines as straight lines (horizontal, vertical or at 45°) and has the stations evenly spaced.
   c) Other designers have used this style when designing maps, e.g. of road networks.

2) a) He wanted to mass-produce products but keep them as stylish and original as possible.
   b) e.g. Philippe Starck

3) a) Designing the road signs that are still used today.
   b) Their style/the typeface/the pictures made the signs easy for drivers to understand.

4) a) Folding and cutting paper to create models that unfold and move.
   b) pop-up books

5) a) The image the public has of a company.
   b) To help people recognise their brand.

c) He's a brand consultant who has helped companies to develop their corporate identity.

6) a) a trademark
   b) registered design
   c) copyright

Page 9 — Design Briefs and Specifications

1) a) E.g. what kind of product is needed, how the product will be used, who the product is for.
   b) the client

2) To find out about what people like/dislike about existing products. To see if people will want your product.

3) E.g. blue is the most popular colour and most people think that the font size is too small.

4) a) A list of conditions that the product must meet.
   b) E.g. how it should look / how it will be used / materials / production method / size / safety points / price range.
   c) E.g. must hold 150 chocolate bars, should have a colourful, shiny surface finish, must have the logo of the chocolate bar, must be no more than 1600 mm tall, must cost less than £4 to manufacture.

Page 11 — Development and Evaluation

1) a) E.g. to check that the shape of the product is how she wanted.
   b) e.g. cardboard, balsa wood or expanded polystyrene
   c) Test that it works how it's supposed to and evaluate it against the design specification.

2) Prototypes are full-size working products made from the right materials, using the right construction methods. Mock-ups are often made from cheap materials and may not have all the working parts.

3) She could test the prototype scales to make sure they work correctly safely. If they do, she could ask some people from her target market to use the scales and give her feedback. If the scales work well and people like them she could consider going into larger scale production. If there are problems or potential customers don't like the scales she would try to fix the problems/ change the design first.

4) a) It tests the product doing its normal job to see how well it works and to make sure it doesn't break.
   b) It helps manufacturers to write safety instructions for their products — e.g. how heavy a load the product can take.

5) Any four from, e.g. Do you like the pop-up features? / What ages do you think they're suitable for? / Do you like the colours? / What don't you like about the cards? / How much would you be willing to pay?

Page 13 — Manufacturing Specification

1) a) A series of written statements, or working drawings and sequence diagrams which explain exactly how to make the product.
   b) Any three from, e.g. materials / tolerances / finishing details / costings / quality control checks / sizes.

2) Working drawings show the design with the precise dimensions, details of materials, etc., marked on.

3) Put the quality control checks in diamond-shaped decision boxes.

Answers

4) a) None of the processes can happen at the same time.
   b) 80 minutes
   c) Applying the writing and logo — it takes 20 minutes.

Page 15 — Paper and Board

1) Bleed-proof paper — the ink doesn't spread out.

2) a) The surface is textured.
   b) It's used for sketching.

3) They're both translucent / they both let light through.

4) gsm (grams per square metre)

5) Duplex board has only one side smooth for printing. It's used in food packaging because it's unbleached.

6) a) Primary packaging is used for individual items. Secondary packaging is used to contain lots of the same item.
   b) Primary packaging — e.g. soft white board.
      Secondary packaging — e.g. corrugated board.

7) Grey board — it's rigid and can be covered with paper for printing.

8) It's often made from recycled paper and can also be recycled itself.

9) A3

Page 17 — Paper and Board

1) It's a sandwich of thin card with polystyrene foam in the middle. It's used for models and mounting posters.

2) a) aluminium
   b) It keeps flavours in and air out.
   c) It's hard to recycle because the paper and aluminium need to be separated first.

3) a) Paper and glue.
   b) They're lightweight and strong.

4) E.g. thick board is stronger so will withstand more bashing about and can take heavier loads. However, it's more expensive and is heavier.

5) cost, quality, flexibility, finish, strength, weight, sustainability

Page 19 — Plastics

1) High impact polystyrene — rigid, cheap, good for vacuum forming. Expanded polystyrene foam — lightweight, good for 3D modelling.

2) Acetate, PVC and corrugated plastic.

3) a) corrugated plastic
   b) expanded polystyrene foam

4) a) acetate
   b) PVC

5) They're made from crude oil which will one day run out/is a finite resource.

Page 21 — Modern and Smart Materials

1) a) cornstarch polymer
   b) potatopak
   c) paper foam

2) Potatopak is made from plants, so it's a renewable material/is sustainable. It's also biodegradable.

3) a) precious metal clay
   b) The clay would be worked into the right shape. Then it is heated to create a solid object. It can then be polished.

4) a) Smart materials react to their environment by changing their properties.
   b) Thermochromic ink — it would change colour as the temperature falls.

Page 23 — Fillers and Finishing

1) e.g. plaster filler

2) Use sandpaper to lightly rub down the surface to give a rough surface. Clean the surface by wiping off any dust. Apply the filler and leave it to dry. Sand the filler back to a smooth flat surface using rough then smooth sandpaper.

3) a) Clean and prime the surface.
   b) e.g. brushes / spray can
   c) Each coat will dry quickly and is less likely to be streaky.

4) He could laminate them or coat them with varnish.

Page 25 — Drawing and Painting

1) a) an HB pencil
   b) e.g. a 2H pencil

2) E.g. chalk pastels — they're good for adding tone and they're easy to blend / coloured pencils — they come in a variety of hardnesses so you can produce different tones of shading.

3) a) set square / protractor
   b) bow compass / beam compass
   c) French curve / flexicurve

4) Draw a straight line. Put your protractor against the line with the cross at the end. Mark a dot next to 50°. Draw a line from the dot to the end of your straight line.

5) Set the arms of your compasses so that they're 30 mm wide.

Page 27 — Adhesives

1) a) e.g. glue stick / glue pen
   b) an aerosol glue
   c) PVA
   d) superglue

2) Make sure the glue doesn't get on to her skin as it's hot.

3) Mix the resin and the hardener together and then apply to the surfaces in a thin layer and stick surfaces together when tacky.

4) a) He could use double-sided tape.
   b) e.g. adhesive plastic film/sticky-backed plastic

Page 29 — Tools

1) a) e.g. a surgical scalpel
   b) compass cutter
   c) e.g. metal-cased knife
   d) rotary cutter or guillotine

2) a) e.g. cutting STYROFOAM™
   b) Cutting out materials for packaging.

3) cutting mat, safety rule

4) Make sure that there's plenty of ventilation and wear a mask.

Page 31 — Fixings and Bindings

1) Any three from, e.g. eyelets / double-sided sticky pads / ratchet rivets / post and screw fixings / snap rivets.

Answers

2) a) e.g. treasury tags / prong paper fasteners
   b) e.g. velcro pads / a hook

3) a) e.g. saddle stitching / comb binding / spiral binding
   b) The pages are less likely to come loose.

Page 33 — Sketching

1) a) When you don't use any drawing equipment apart from a pencil/pen.
   b) Sketching initial design ideas.
   c) To explain details further, e.g. ideas for colours/materials.

2)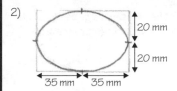

3) a)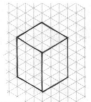
   b) E.g. perspective grid / square grid

4) a) Crating is where you start by drawing a box and gradually add bits on and take bits off till you get the right shape.
   b) e.g.
   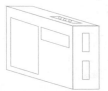 
   c) wireframe drawings

Page 35 — Shading and Texture

1)   2)

3) E.g. use coloured pencils — use more than one colour to get the right shade and use a darker colour to show the grain.

4) highlights

5) a) Any two from, e.g. marker pens / coloured pencils / poster paints.
   b) Use water colour paints and add a bit of yellow.

Page 37 — Colour and Mood

1) a) primary and secondary colours
   b) primary — red, blue, yellow.
      secondary — orange, purple, green

2) a) red and blue
   b) yellow and blue

3) a) How light or dark it is.
   b) By adding more black or white.

4) a) Use pale colours.
   b) Any two from, e.g. blue / purple / brown / grey / green.
   c) Red often symbolises danger.

Page 39 — Colour Fusion and Separation

1) a) cyan, magenta, yellow, black
   b) They add layers of cyan, magenta, yellow and black to create other colours.
   c) To make the image look more realistic, e.g. flesh tones and metallic colours. / To make sure that a colour always prints out exactly the same on any printer.

2) a) He would put a stencil of the design under the mesh, and the towel under the stencil.
   b) He'd put dye cream onto the mesh, then pull across a rubber squeegee to push the dye through the mesh and stencil.

3) a) This is when tiny dots of different colours really close together appear to blend into a new, single colour.
   b) Any two from, e.g. posters / leaflets / newspapers.

4) The screen is made up of thousands of tiny coloured pixels. Each pixel consists of a red, green and blue bar. The intensity of each of these bars produces the final pixel colour you see.

5) It separates the image into red, green and blue by taking three pictures at the same time, each using a different colour filter.

Page 41 — Lettering and Presentation

1) a) Presentation drawings are used to show the design idea to the client.
   b) e.g. 3D drawings, working drawings

2) The designer would need to re-draw it if the client wanted any changes making.

3) Any two from, e.g. alter colours / add light and shadow effects / enlarge or reduce / copy and paste / rotate.

4) E.g. they can be distorted, they can be made to look like pencil drawings.

5) a) serif
   b) sans serif
   c) serif

6) E.g. a serif font, to make the brochure look old-fashioned.

7) e.g. a laser cutter

8) a) encapsulation
   b) The menu would be laid between two sheets of clear plastic. This is then inserted into the laminating machine, which heats the plastic and seals the edges around the paper.

Page 43 — Pictorial Drawings

1) Any two from, e.g. pictorial drawing / perspective drawing / isometric drawing.

2) A point in the distance on the horizon line where 'parallel' lines appear to meet.

3) a) e.g.   b) e.g.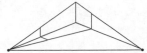

4) 30°

5) a) isometric drawing

Answers

b)

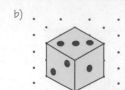

Page 45 — Working Drawings

1) millimetres / mm

2) Front view, plan view and end view.

3) a) exploded views
   b) They clearly show how the different parts should be assembled.

4) a) a sectional drawing
   b) and c) E.g.

5) B

Page 47 — Working Drawings

1) They're used to draw objects either smaller or bigger than they actually are, but keeping all the proportions correct.

2) a) The drawing is a quarter of the size of the real fish.
   b) 40 mm. (Height on drawing = 10 mm. 10 mm × 4 = 40 mm.)

3) e.g.

4) a) A room plan is a scale drawing of a room from above.
   b) E.g. fire escape plans, so people can see the layout of the building.
   c) So that builders can see what they're going to build where.

5) a)

   b) Any suitable answer, e.g. it shows which bus stops come next in a clear and simple order. It's much quicker and easier to read than the geographical map because there is less information to take in.

Page 49 — Nets and Packaging

1) a) A 2D plan for making a 3D object.
   b) A surface development.
   c) My Mum. (Other answers are possible.)

2) They can be used to produce 3D models quickly and cheaply.

3) a) Drawing should show a cuboid structure with an open top, e.g.

   b) You cut along these lines.
   c) You score and fold along these lines.

4) E.g.

5) Any three from, e.g. CAD lets you make your design bigger or smaller but keep the proportions the same / you can rotate and flip your drawing using CAD / you can make complicated designs quickly / you can copy and paste lots of the same net onto one sheet to quickly produce lots of the same net.

6) a) Computer Aided Manufacture
   b) It presses out your net from the sheet material using a blade specially shaped to the outline of your net (and adds creases using a creasing bar).
   c) Die cutting is expensive (because you need to make a blade to match your net).

Page 51 — Charts and Graphs

1) Bar charts use bars to represent information but pictographs use simple pictures/symbols.

2) 100%

3) a) A diagram which shows events in the order they take place.
   b) Quality control during manufacture / to fix problems.

4) a) A series of pictures showing you how to do something.
   b) e.g. flat-pack furniture

5) a) E.g.

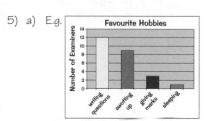

   b) E.g.

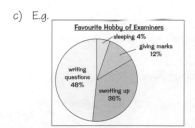

   c) E.g.

   d) E.g. bar chart or pie chart because it's easy to compare the results / pictograph because the information looks interesting.
   e) It can't be plotted in a line graph because the data is not continuous.

Answers

Page 53 — Signs and Labels

1) Small pictures that are used as labels, e.g. the text tool or print symbol in computer software.

2) Ideograms / pictograms

3) a) e.g. CE mark, British Standards Kitemark
   b) e.g. the recycling symbol

4) Any two from, e.g. symbol to show the food is suitable for vegetarians / symbol to show that there's an allergy risk / 'e' symbol for weight or volume.

5) a) e.g.

   b) e.g.

Page 55 — Branding and Social Responsibility

1) a) So that customers can recognise their products.
   b) E.g. the name of the company is clear, and it's clear what the company sells.

2) a) The image that people have of the company.
   b) E.g.

3) a) E.g. they could use recycled materials / biodegradable materials / recyclable materials
   b) E.g. the working conditions might be dangerous / the manufacturing process might harm the environment, e.g. by using up finite resources or producing a lot of waste.

4) E.g. some cultures frown upon women showing any skin. Some cultures find certain colours bad luck, e.g. in China, black is thought to bring bad luck.

Page 57 — Packaging and Sustainability

1) Packaging can protect items when they're being transported / allows products to be stacked neatly and safely in warehouses.

2) Well-designed packaging helps customers to easily find what they want. It can also make it clear what the product is and entice people to buy it. Well-designed packaging can make products stand out from the others.

3) Any two from, e.g. the final cost of the product will be increased / some consumers may be put off buying the product if they think there's too much packaging / there is extra waste / more finite resources are used up.

4) a) They could use designs for the nets that will tessellate and produce less waste. / They could avoid unnecessary packaging.
   b) They might be able to use a less harmful production process or use a biodegradable material for the packaging.

5) Advantage — it means that new products don't need to be made.
   Disadvantage — products often need transporting and cleaning before they can be re-used.

Page 59 — Legal Issues and Standards

1) Written, drawn and recorded work.

2) The symbol, logo, words or slogans that a company uses to represent itself

3) a) registered design
   b) up to 25 years

4) Products that are inventive and could have an industrial application.

5) The Sale of Goods Act — you'd expect a tent to keep water out.

6) Control of Substances Hazardous to Health — it protects people from the effects of hazardous substances, materials and processes.

7) a) Kitemark
   b) The product has met standards set by the British Standards Institution.

8) The product has met EU standards for safety.

Page 61 — Health and Safety

1) a) It ensures that employers provide their employees with a safe working environment, e.g. by using safety signs.
   b) They examine workplaces to check that rules and regulations are being followed.

2) E.g. he should use a safety rule and a cutting mat, and secure the card before cutting.

3) Make sure there's adequate ventilation.

4) E.g. know how to switch the machine off and isolate it / don't leave the machine unattended while it's switched on / secure the work safely / keep flammable substances away from the machine.

5) a) A risk assessment is an evaluation carried out to identify and minimise any potential risks.
   b) The MDF could slip — make sure it's clamped before cutting.
   Sawdust could get into eyes — wear safety goggles.
   Clothing could get caught — roll sleeves back, wear an apron.
   The MDF could be left with sharp edges after cutting — sand down any rough edges.
   The saw could 'jump' and cause injuries — keep free hand well away from the saw.

Page 63 — CAD/CAM

1) a) e.g. Pro/DESKTOP®
   b) E.g. you can change your design quickly / it's easy to experiment with alternative colours and forms / you can spot any problems before you make your product.

2) a) Computer Aided Manufacture.
   b) The machines follow the x,y,z coordinates from the CAD software, and move the tools to shape the material.

3) a) Any three from, e.g. it's easy to develop, edit and experiment with the design / you can produce realistic designs / you can manufacture loads of products in a short amount of time / you get a high quality and a more reliable finished product / money is saved because labour costs are lower.
   b) Any two from, e.g. the software and hardware is expensive / workers need lots of training, which is expensive / work can be disrupted by computer viruses/corrupt files.

4) He would draw the design using CAD. The software turns this into numerical instructions telling a CAM milling machine how far to move in each direction to shape the plastic.

Answers

Page 65 — ICT

1) a) All the computer equipment that's hard/that you can physically move about.
   b) computer programs
2) To work out production costs / time management.
3) a) Equipment you use to transfer information/pictures onto a computer.
   b) Equipment you use to transfer data out of a computer (as a 'hard copy' or product).
4) a) E.g. she could use a graphics tablet to write her name.
   b) E.g. she could use a digital camera to take a photo of herself and download this to a computer / she could use a scanner to scan in a picture of herself.
5) The designer can work in one location and easily transfer the work to the client in a different location. The designs can be sent as attachments via email, and discussed over the phone. Meetings can be held using teleconferencing. This would help the project move quickly and makes sure the final product turns out exactly how the client wants it to be.

Page 67 — Systems and Quality Control

1) A collection of parts that work together to do a particular function.
2) Inputs, processes and outputs.
3) He can show the stages of the manufacturing process in the right order and include quality checks.
4)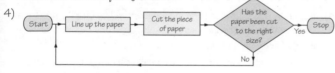
5) They make sure that the product meets the manufacturing specification, functions properly, conforms to quality and safety standards and is manufactured consistently.
6) a) 146 mm by 96 mm
   b) 154 mm by 104 mm

Page 69 — Scale of Production

1) Advantage — e.g. you can meet a customer's exact requirements. Disadvantage — e.g. it's labour intensive / expensive
2) a) Making a set number of the same product .
   b) E.g. leaflets, brochures, posters.
3) a) The equipment is very expensive so you need to make money back by selling loads of your product.
   b) The staff don't need to be as highly skilled.
4) e.g. food packaging
5) a) A just-in-time system is where the manufacturer gets the materials and components delivered as they're needed and uses them as soon as they're delivered.
   b) E.g. because it saves on space for storing materials / there's less money tied up in materials that aren't being used / unsold finished products don't pile up.
6) E.g. he might need to change his equipment / he might need to change the order he does things to make the process as efficient as possible.

Page 71 — Packaging and Mechanisms

1) E.g. the trays in mobile phone packaging.
2) a) Blow moulding works by inserting a tube of softened plastic into a solid mould and injecting air so the plastic expands to the shape of the mould.
   b) e.g. milk bottles / plastic bottles
3) a) He could produce a net of the display stand then make blades for the die cutter to match the outline of the net. Then he'd mount the die cutter on a strong backing and press it down onto several of layers of card to cut out lots of nets at once.
   b) E.g. they could be used to play music, or make parts of the display light up.

Page 73 — Printing — Commercial Methods

1) Ultraviolet light is used to transfer the image onto a smooth aluminium printing plate — the image area gets coated with a chemical that attracts the oily ink but repels water. So the image area holds ink and the non-image area holds water.
2) E.g. the surface you're printing on doesn't need to be flat / it's quicker than lithography / the plates are long-lasting.
3) Gravure is a high quality printing method that uses an etched brass printing plate.
4) You put a stencil under a fine mesh screen and spread ink over the top. The ink goes through the stencil and prints onto the material.
5) a) Inkjet and laser printers.
   b) Apart from buying the printer there are no set-up costs.
6) a) E.g. lithography because it's high-quality and good for print runs of 1000 copies or more.
   b) Screen printing — it can print on fabric.
   c) Flexography — it can print onto curved surfaces.
   d) Gravure — you get very high-quality printing.

Page 75 — Printing Quality and Finishes

1) A colour registration mark. It's used by printers to check the printing plates are aligned in the right position.
2) Colour bars are used to check the density of colours being printed and to check they match the exact colours of the image.
3) a) Crop marks show where an image needs to be cut to size.
   b) The bleed area is a bit of extra printing around the crop marks to ensure that there are no white edges (even if the sheet is cut slightly too large).
4) a) The product will look smooth, glossy and higher quality.
   b) The product will last longer without getting damaged.
   c) Embossing draws attention to a particular bit of the product and can suggest quality.
   d) Foil application draws attention to a particular bit of the product, e.g. a logo. It can suggest quality.

Page 77 — Production Methods

1) They save time/speed up work and ensure consistency.
2) Because they're used over and over again.
3) It guides the tool and makes sure that every component is identical.
4) If only a small number of products are needed.
5) a) To save money and to reduce harm to the environment.
   b) Tessellating means fitting shapes together so that there aren't any gaps / so that as many shapes as possible fit on one sheet of material.

Index

Index